WHAT CHRIST...
ARE SAYIN...
CUTTING... P9-CQO-327

"The sickness of American public schools has metastasized to the church. The result—nobody learns much of anything. Fortunately, [this] book is not short of solutions, and the [accompanying] video shows several teachers creatively helping their students *learn* biblical truth."
Leadership Journal

"Nowhere is educational reform more needed than in the church. This book arouses enthusiasm for the task. It's a refreshing call to active learning and a practical manual for renewing the education program of a local church."
Thomas A. Fleming
Former National Teacher of the Year

"Not only have Thom and Joani Schultz identified the major roadblocks in the way of effective ministry, they have prescribed practical, innovative, and constructive solutions. This is one of those rare books to which you'll refer again and again and again—one of those books you'll want everyone who is involved in the church to read."
Guy Doud
Former National Teacher of the Year

"...Provides a roadmap for energizing lagging Christian education and solid learning of the faith in an age of boredom and ineffective teaching. Thom and Joani Schultz move beyond theory to practice."
Russell Chandler
Author, speaker
Former Religion Writer, The Los Angeles Times

"Thom and Joani Schultz carefully take the reader through the reasons WHY traditional teaching is not working...They provide an alternative that is biblically based and proven to be far more effective in helping people internalize and apply what they're learning."
Jody Capehart
Christian Educator
*Author, **Becoming a Treasured Teacher***

"I have to list this book as one of the top resources *every* Christian educator should possess—from Sunday School teacher to seminary instructor."
Richard Chromey
Professor of Christian Education & Youth Ministry
Boise Bible College

"...biblically based, intensely practical, and developed out of extensive research and experience...This reviewer strongly recommends that pastors, teachers, Christian educators, youth workers, and all others who are involved in the Christian education program of the church get a copy of this book, read it, and take it to heart."
Covenanter Witness

"Each teacher and pastor should read this timely work."
Regular Baptist Press

"Very clear and exceptionally practical. Anyone who implements the principles the authors outline will definitely make giant steps in improving their teaching. I recommend the book."
Michael S. Lawson, Ph.D.
BIB SAC Review

"...This book has been long past due...thanks for your boldness in writing what I have been thinking for a long time."
Pete Brissette
Sunday School Director

"I recommend this book and the accompanying video to those Christian educators who are seeking to renew the local church educational program."
J. T. Hammond, Ed.D.
"ExCEllence"
Messenger

"[This book] makes a significant contribution to the improvement of education in our churches and underscores the importance of education that leads to changed lives, rather than merely acquiring facts and information."
Dennis E. Williams
Professor of Christian Education
Denver Seminary

"With a format that is readily adaptable to teacher training, *Why Nobody Learns Much*...offers practical, usable, and imaginative methods. Some of the strengths of this book are its common-sense approach to learning and its usefulness as a training tool."
Phil Baisley
Resources

"Students enjoy using the book because it's reality driven and focused on the present situation most are facing in their churches. I like the book because it reinforces a number of ideas I have had concerning C.E. at the local church level. I am also using the book as a resource in my youth ministries class...I am also recommending the book to pastors as a resource for improving their own teaching in the church. This book will remain a required textbook in future classes."
Mike Thompson
Assistant Professor of Church Ministries
Northwest College

A 1994 GOLD MEDALLION AWARD FINALIST

WHY NOBODY LEARNS MUCH OF ANYTHING AT CHURCH:
And How to Fix It

By Thom and Joani Schultz

Group
Loveland, Colorado

Dedication

We dedicate this book to our son, Matt,
whose zest for learning inspires us both!

TABLE OF CONTENTS

5.99

93293

Introduction

THE LOST ART OF LEARNING IN THE CHURCH

We spend a good deal of time talking with kids. Not long ago we talked with dozens of fifth- and sixth-grade kids about their learning experiences at church. We'll let you eavesdrop on one of those conversations:

Thom: How long have you been going to church?

Katrina: Since I was a baby.

Thom: How do you like your classes at church?

Katrina: They're too much like school.

Thom: How's that?

Katrina: They're boring.

Thom: How so?

Katrina: We have to sit in chairs and memorize stuff.

Thom: What have you memorized?

Katrina: Verses from the Bible. We get a piece of candy if we come with verses memorized.

Thom: Can you say the last verse you got some candy for?

Katrina: I don't remember.

Thom: Do you remember any of them?

Katrina: No, I'm sorry.

Thom: Well, can you remember what any of them meant?

Katrina: No. I guess I have a bad memory.

Thom: Katrina, can you tell me what it takes for a person to get to heaven?

Katrina: Study hard.

Is Katrina unusual? Or is she a typical product of the church's teaching efforts?

Our temptation is to dismiss Katrina as a to-be-expected laggard. "Some people just don't do as well as others," we say. "Besides, she's learning good things. She just doesn't know it. It'll all come back to her someday."

We're an optimistic lot. And we've been doing the same things for so long we don't spend a lot of time wondering about their effectiveness. We're too busy doing what we're doing to question if what we're doing is working.

Well, is the learning enterprise working in the church? Are we getting a decent return on our substantial investment in religious education, Sunday school, Bible studies, youth groups, children's programs, confirmation and discipleship classes, vacation Bible school, adult classes, and sermon times? Let's look at some indicators.

SIGNS OF A SINKING SHIP

● Out of a whole host of church attributes, church-attenders rank the church's teaching at the bottom of the quality scale. Only youth programs receive a poorer grade, according to researcher George Barna.[1]

● Since 1972 Sunday school attendance has dropped from 41 million to 26 million, according to the *Yearbook of American and Canadian Churches.* During the same period the general U.S. population grew by 23 percent.[2]

● Church school participation in mainline denominations declined an average of 55 percent between 1970 and 1990.[3]

● The number of churches that even offer Sunday school declined 43 percent during the '80s.[4]

● Only 19 percent of churchgoing adults say they usually learn a lot from their pastors' sermons.[5]

WORDS OF WARNING

Have these trends gone completely unnoticed? Well, not completely. A few well-informed voices have been trying to get our attention:

"Christian education in a majority of congregations is a tired enterprise in need of reform. Often out of touch with adult and adolescent needs, it experiences increasing difficulty in finding and motivating volunteers, faces general disinterest among its 'clients,' and employs models and procedures that have changed little over time."

—*Peter Benson and Carolyn Eklin,
Search Institute* [6]

> **"Sunday schools simply do not provide
> the quality of teaching and experience
> that people demand these days in
> exchange for their time."**
> —*George Barna, researcher* [7]

> **"The Sunday school ... is increasingly
> archaic in a time when family
> patterns have changed."**
> —*Robert Lynn, Lilly Endowment* [8]

> **"The teachers just talk and
> we just sit there."**
> —*Brian, third-grader* [9]

WHAT'S THE BIG DEAL?

"All right, all right," you say. "So what if the church is a little weak in education? It's not the end of the world."

Don't be so sure. The latest studies indicate that education can be the church's most potent tool for growing its people's faith. Search Institute surveyed over 11,000 adults and youth in churches of several denominations. Upon completion of the study, researchers Peter Benson and Carolyn Eklin said, "Christian education matters much more than we expected. Of all the areas of congregational life we examined, involvement in an effective Christian education program has the strongest tie to a person's growth in faith. While other congregational factors also matter, nothing matters more than effective Christian education. And this is as true for adults as it is for adolescents."[10]

If our people aren't learning, they're not growing in their faith. And, sadly, we have ample evidence that our people aren't learning much. What they *are* learning isn't always what we think we're teaching. Katrina's plan of salvation ("study hard") is but one example.

The problem of learning in the church is a monumental one. It's at the core of those churches in membership decline. It's what's undermining the church's influence on our society. It's the root cause of member apathy. It's causing our kids to yawn at Jesus.

We're all victims of an outdated educational system. No one has intentionally sabotaged learning in the church. Ineffective teaching methods have been passed down from generation to generation. And we've continued to use them—with all good intentions.

BUT IS THERE ANY HOPE?

After listening to our concern about learning in the church, an executive from a Christian curriculum publishing house said, "The fact that kids say they can't remember any lessons from Sunday school doesn't surprise me. I think if you'd ask kids about public school, you'd get the same answer."

Should that give us great comfort? So long as the public schools produce substandard results, that gives us license to sit and bask in our own poor performance? We can, and should, do better.

It is true the church isn't the only old institution with a crisis in learning. Our public schools are also in big trouble.

**A recent World Competitiveness
Report rated the United States 21st in
the world in educational quality,
trailed only by Greece among industrialized nations.[11]**

Our public school kids aren't learning at an accept-
able rate. And they're no more fond of the process than
our church kids. An average of 3,878 teenagers drop out
of public school every day. An estimated one million
students drop out every year.[12]

"The students in our nation's schools are substantial-
ly different individuals from the students of 10, 20, and
30 years ago," says Tony Carvajal, director of the Center
for the Interdisciplinary Study of Dropout Prevention.
"The teaching methods of yesterday don't address the
needs of today's students."

But neither the public schools nor the church is left
without solutions to this big problem. Carvajal says, "To
reach the students of today, the curriculum must actively
engage the learners and promote higher-order thinking
instead of merely memorization of facts and figures."

Public schools are beginning to wake up to the need
for change—real change. And where they're risking
new approaches to learning, they're seeing some break-
through successes that will serve as models for schools
in the next century. In progressive schools, educators are
emphasizing active learning by the students. Teachers
are de-emphasizing lecture-style pedagogy, rote memorization, and textbook-based classrooms. They're teaching kids to think, to problem-solve.

And students are learning.

> **"A new wave of teachers is casting out textbooks, cursing standardized tests, killing drills, and preaching a new creed of student 'engagement.'"**
>
> —*The Wall Street Journal* [13]

"Well, the church isn't the public school," you say. No, it isn't. But we can benefit from listening to the best thinkers in education today. Some tremendously effective new models are emerging that we can use in the church. We'll share those with you in the pages to come.

And we'll share with you innovative approaches to learning that we've used successfully in churches over the past 20 years. No pie-in-the-sky stuff. But solid, creative approaches that work.

Join us as we explore 10 keys to help you unlock learning in the church.

> **"Show me your ways, O Lord;**
> **teach me your paths."**
>
> —*Psalm 25:4, NIV*

1 KNOW THE GOAL

So there's a big problem with learning in the church. Who or what is to blame? We've heard a plethora of answers:

- "Teachers are everything. But nobody wants to teach anymore."
- "This generation of parents just doesn't care about kids."
- "Television is ruining everybody. Nobody likes real education because they expect it to be like TV."
- "People's priorities are messed up. They just don't care about spiritual things anymore."
- "People are too busy."
- "We don't have the budget to do a good job."
- "Women in the workplace have robbed us of all our decent teachers."
- "Kids today are too wild and unruly to learn anything."
- "People come to church too sporadically."
- "Education in the church has an image problem. What we need is a public relations campaign! How about if we print up bumper stickers that say, 'I Love Sunday School'?"

I ♥ SUNDAY SCHOOL

Well, education in the church does indeed have an image problem. Unfortunately, the public's image is pretty accurate. And applying happy bumper stickers won't change an unhappy situation. Pasting a new label onto an old, worn-out battery won't help your car start on a cold morning.

No, the problem isn't a public relations one. And it's none of those other problems previously suggested. The problem is far more basic.

The problem is:

> **We've lost our way.**
> **We've forgotten why we're**
> **doing what we're doing.**

MISGUIDED BAROMETERS

We've become so busy doing the same things over and over that we've lost sight of the goal. The overriding goal of education in the church has been rusted over by expectations that few have bothered to stop to evaluate. And these expectations have frequently become the misguided barometers and goals of the church's educational efforts. Some examples:

● *"The kids keep coming."* Is a body in a chair the net result of Christian education? Are we no more than a convenient drop-off zone for parents on their way to Sunday morning doughnuts? Attendance is fine. In fact, it's usually a prerequisite for learning. But attendance does not ensure learning. Attendance is not the goal.

● *"Our classrooms are well-disciplined and quiet."* Silence and passivity in a classroom usually indicate a lack of learning. Passive kids or adults sitting quietly while the teacher imparts his or her knowledge may make the teacher feel great, but are we certain anyone is learning anything? Discipline and silence are not the goal.

- *"Our teenagers really love our youth pastor."* That can be positive sometimes. It may help your kids be receptive to real learning—if your youth pastor takes that receptiveness beyond adulation. But adoration of staff is not the goal.

- *"We're using this theologically correct material."* Good theology is good. But good medicine matters only if someone swallows it and is healed. Our educational efforts must be both theologically sound and result in actual life-changing learning. Theologically correct curriculum is not the goal.

- *"We like our curriculum because the profits go toward the denomination's pastor pension fund."* Planning for retirement is prudent. But would you choose a school for your kids based on how the principal's pension plans were funded? Your kids' education is too important. Publishing house profits and pensions are not the goal.

- *"Our teachers have no complaints with the material we're using."* Is that the goal? Imagine if your church's restroom floors always appeared grimy, even immediately after the custodian mopped. Upon inquiry, would you be satisfied if the custodian simply shrugged and said, "The cleanser I use seems fine to me"? No, you'd want results. Teacher acquiescence is not the goal.

- *"The children are busy the whole hour."* Were they punching out those little stickers to paste on the take-home papers? Were they toiling over another set of Bible word-scrambles? Is our goal merely to fill time—or to encourage life-changing learning? Busyness is not the goal.

- *"We believe in strong Bible teaching."* But do you care about strong Bible learning? If a political candidate makes fiery speeches but receives no votes, what is gained? Teaching is not the goal.

● *"Our Bible quiz team wins every time."* Memorization of Bible facts may win contests. But does it result in the kind of learning that Jesus produced among his followers? Memorization of facts is not the goal.

● *"We teach our denomination's history and foundations."* That's fine, unless your students fail to learn the bigger lesson. What would it matter if a Boy Scout knew the date when the scouting movement began, who started it, where it originated—if he did not learn to always "be prepared" in real life? Sectarian historical knowledge is not the goal.

● *"Our kids are earning lots of incentive awards."* Many churches dish out rewards for attendance, bringing visitors, completing assignments, memorizing verses. But that's teaching kids to focus on the grade rather than the process of real learning. Winning stickers, stars, and bribes is not the goal.

● *"Our pastor is a good speaker."* Sending a good message is important. Writing a fine recipe is a good accomplishment. But the cook is not truly successful until someone takes the recipe and makes a good stew. Good speaking is not the goal.

The preceding quotes represent a misguided church. While the church's keepers wander in the wilderness of forgotten goals, millions of children, youth, and adults wallow in spiritual malnourishment. Is this famine intentional? Of course not. The body of Christ has the best of intentions. But time, tradition, and busyness have dulled our senses and crippled our better judgment.

The church is not alone in the forgotten-goal quagmire. Goal confusion is really quite common. For instance, take the case of one of our local restaurants. We took 18 of our staff members to lunch to celebrate a project's completion. The service was very poor. Our anticipated one-hour lunch extended beyond two hours. Our afternoon appointments were dashed. We complained to the restaurant's owner-cook. She refused to adjust the bill, offer any other compensation, or even apologize. She insisted on payment in full, even though she knew 18 good customers were most unhappy.

She forgot her goal. You see, she mistakenly thought her goal was to collect—in full—every customer's check. But the real goal of any restaurant is to build a consistent and lucrative repeat business. That owner's misguided behavior resulted in 18 people who paid their bills in full, but who will never return to that restaurant.

LOST GOALS IN THE SCHOOLS

America's schools provide another example of forgotten goals. The schools have become preoccupied with uniformity, standardized tests, fill-in-the-blanks, and a factory approach to education. They've forgotten the real goal of education—to help prepare kids for the real world and inspire them to become lifelong learners.

"The problem is fundamental. Put 20 or more children of roughly the same age in a little room, confine them to desks, make them behave. It is as if a secret committee, now lost to history,

**had made a study of children and, hav-
ing figured out what the greatest number were least disposed to do, declared
that all of them should do it."**

—Tracy Kidder, journalist [1]

In an effort to "get back to basics," some schools have
bulldozed right over the true basics. Take the school in
Ohio where teachers have been handed 230 "pupil performance objectives" in the area of reading alone. Not
one of these objectives deals with the goal that children
might learn to love books.[2]

Is anyone checking with the customers of this high-tick-
et item called public education? Are our kids graduating
with the skills and experiences that will adequately enhance
their lives in our rapidly changing world? Or are they leaving school simply knowing how to cram for a test?

We have an antiquated school regime built around the
farm calendar—summers off for work in the fields. But
we don't understand the most basic law of the farm. The
harvest is what really matters. And the harvest won't come
unless the farmer believes in and tends to the process—
preparing the soil, planting, fertilizing, weeding, and then
harvesting. It takes time and care. The farmer knows that
cramming won't work. If he or she pays no attention to the
process but tries to cram and plant a week before the harvest, it'll be a mighty slim winter.

Yet our system has taught kids that cramming works.
All that counts is that grade on the exam. Stuff your head
with short-term facts and figures, learn how to select best-
guess answers on a multiple-choice exam, outsmart the
system. And settle for a grade rather than an education.

**"The tests the students have to take are
geared to the textbooks, the textbooks
are boring, below the kids' abilities,
and geared to workbook sheets and dit-
tos. My administrator wants high test
scores because they make the school—
him, really—look good. Any space I
can find to really get kids involved in
class, to really cut loose on a project,
shrinks almost every day."**

—*Elementary school teacher* [3]

One of the saddest commentaries on our educational system comes from John Taylor Gatto, who was the New York State Teacher of the Year in 1991:

"I've come slowly to understand what it is I really teach: a curriculum of confusion, class position, arbitrary justice, vulgarity, rudeness, disrespect for privacy, indifference to quality, and utter dependency. I teach how to fit into a world I don't want to live in.

"My orders as schoolteacher are to make children fit an animal training system, not to help each find his or her personal path."[4]

**"Teaching has not changed notably
in the 24 years that I have been
teaching. Somewhere along the line
we've missed the idea or the vision
of what education is all about. The**

whole system is outdated."

*—Deanna Woods, high school
teacher in Portland, Oregon* [5]

George H. Wood sums it up in his book *Schools That Work:* "For decades Americans believed that big equals better, that coverage equals knowledge, that schools should work like factories, both administratively and ped-agogically. We have accepted virtually without question the way schools currently look and operate. It's as if schools in their structure and form but not their output are sacred and beyond question." [6]

Schools have lost sight of the goal. They've forgotten that the harvest is the only goal that really matters. They've been lulled into believing that driving old tractors to and fro is the goal of the farm. They've taken their eye off the harvest. Unfortunately the church has plowed the same field.

RUN STRAIGHT TOWARD THE GOAL

Paul wrote to the Philippians, "I do not claim that I have already succeeded in this, or have already become perfect. I keep going on to try to possess it, for Christ Jesus has already possessed me. Of course, I really do not think that I have already reached it; my single purpose in life, however, is to forget what is behind me and do my best to reach what is ahead. So I run straight toward the goal in order to win the prize, which is God's call through Christ Jesus to the life above" (Philippians 3:12-14, TEV).

> **"If you know where you want to go,
> you have a much better chance
> of getting there."**
>
> —*Anonymous*

Look at the illustration below. Study it carefully. What do you see?

When the face in the drawing looks to the right it is a rabbit. When the face looks left it's a duck. Depending on which face you focus on, you can imagine the whole body below the neck. But can you see both animals at once? It's very difficult. Our attention tends to favor one over the other.

The battle is on for our attention in the church. What will be our real focus? Without a clearly defined goal we'll waffle and never "win the prize." But if our educational goal is a good one that's apparent to everyone, we'll change lives with the power of the Lord.

So what's the goal? Let's look to our people—and to God's Word.

Today's teenagers, children, and adults come to church with some very basic educational needs. They hunger for the gospel.

A Search Institute study found that only 11 percent of churchgoing teenagers have a well-developed faith. The

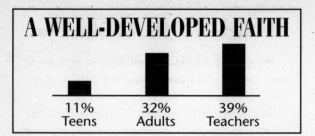

A WELL-DEVELOPED FAITH

| 11% | 32% | 39% |
| Teens | Adults | Teachers |

figure rises to only 32 percent for churchgoing adults, and to 39 percent for Christian education teachers.[7]

The same study revealed what adults and adolescents most want to learn about at church. You'll notice that basic faith issues are a high priority for both adults and teenagers.

ADULTS WANT TO LEARN ABOUT
1. The Bible.
2. Developing a personal relationship with Jesus.
3. Improving skills at showing love and concern.

TEENAGERS WANT TO LEARN ABOUT
1. Knowing how to make friends and be a friend.
2. Learning to know and love Jesus Christ.
3. Learning more about who God is.[8]

And, finally, Jesus' two great commandments help guide our learning goal: "Love the Lord your God with all your heart, all your soul, and all your mind" and "Love your neighbor as you love yourself" (Matthew 22:37-39).

OUR GOAL

We've settled on "to know, love, and follow Jesus" as our own goal for learning in the church. It covers the cognitive, the affective, and the behavioral. It's results-orient-

EVIDENCE OF LEARNING

Which of the following would best indicate to you that a student has learned the parable of the Good Samaritan?

A. The student memorizes and recites the entire parable word for word from your preferred translation.

B. The student tells the parable in his or her own words.

C. The student explains an example of someone being a "good Samaritan."

D. The student decides to sit and have lunch with an outcast kid who's rumored to have AIDS.

---

ed, harvest-oriented. It reminds us that Christianity is a lifestyle. And, as educators, we're successful only when our students' learning results in real-life action, in changed lives.

One life that was changed by properly aligned goals is Joani's. She grew up in rural South Dakota and attended a tiny church pastored by the Rev. Keith Johnson. This country pastor knew his goals. Even though Joani was often the only teenager to show up, Johnson carried out his youth ministry plans. While many would have canceled their youth group activities with only one attender, Johnson knew his goal was not an arbitrary attendance figure. The goal was spiritual growth. Johnson's untiring devotion to the real goal resulted in a girl devoting her life to full-time Christian service.

If we produce those kinds of results, many of the problems cited at the beginning of this chapter will take care of themselves. You complain about today's volunteers and parents? If today's baby-boomer parents saw evidence of quality—that is, if they perceived that their church produced any net effect in their children's spiritual growth—they'd gladly volunteer their precious time to help. And if the church's adult classes really affected people's lives, the classes would be brimming. Currently only 23 percent of churchgoing adults typically attend any weekly class.[9]

So what's *your* goal? If a succinct goal doesn't immediately come to mind, it's time to construct one. Then measure everything you do against it. Be prepared to throw out any beliefs and approaches that are consuming valuable time which could be spent on more direct progress toward your goal.

The next section will help you determine and put into action your church's goal for learning.

A GOAL
"Love the Lord your God with all your heart, all your soul, and all your strength."
—Deuteronomy 6:5

At the end of each chapter you'll find a "Do It" section with practical programming ideas to help you share and apply these principles in your church.

Well, you're ready to consider some changes. But where do you begin? Here's a step-by-step plan for goal-setting that will help set the vision for your congregation's education ministry. It incorporates some of the principles found in future chapters of this book.

Here's a starting place. Ready? Set? Goal!

CRAFTING YOUR GOAL

1. Gather together people who care about education. Select a cross-section of key people—the obvious and not-so-obvious. The number can vary from three to 10 (or more). Just remember that the larger the group, the longer it will take. And that's okay. The smaller the group, the quicker.

Invite the obvious:
● Sunday school teachers
● adult education teachers
● church staff members
● education administrator (Sunday school superintendent or organizer)

Remember the not-so-obvious:
● concerned parents
● teenagers
● young adults
● public school educators
● children (if you're willing to listen to them!)

It's important to remember that *everyone* has some sort of base-level experience with "school"—

whether it's public or Christian education. Most of us have been "taught" in a classroom and have valuable insights to contribute from past experiences.

One reminder: Work through the proper church channels. Get the leadership on board. There's nothing more frustrating than getting revved up about change and then being stonewalled because you didn't connect with the people "in charge."

2. Meet together to raise concerns and do goal-setting. Here's where the fun begins! Try the 2½ hour meeting agenda that follows. There's a lot to cover, so pace yourself. Be a good timekeeper.

A MEETING AGENDA FOR GOAL-SETTING

GETTING STARTED

❏ Welcome people and thank them for taking time to explore the issue of learning at your church.

❏ Pray for guidance and wisdom as you work together to set your goal for learning.

❏ Tell the group why you're interested in digging into your church's education efforts. Briefly share a couple of highlights from this book that particularly intrigued you and motivated you to gather this group.

❏ Have people introduce themselves and tell about a significant memory they have from church or Sunday school.

A VIDEO PEEK

If you'd like to meet some real-live people we interviewed about learning in the church, use the 35-minute video also called *Why Nobody Learns Much of Anything at Church,* available from Group Publishing.

It's a fascinating peek at what children, youth, and adults perceive about teaching and learning. Use it to sensitize your goal-setting team to the issues. Then show it to spark intrigue among congregation members as you focus on the goal.

❑ Introduce the topic of learning in the church. Have two volunteers play the part of Thom and Katrina from the dialogue on pages 7 and 8.

❑ If the group is larger than six, form smaller groups to discuss:

● **What feelings did you have after hearing that conversation?**

● **How is that like or unlike what you think most young people would say?**

● **Why do you think Katrina answered the way she did?**

❑ If you formed small groups, have people report back what they discussed in their groups.

❑ Post five sheets of paper on the wall, each containing one of the five bulleted items from the "Signs of a Sinking Ship" section on page 8. Invite people to wander around and read each sheet. Have them stand next to the statistic that surprises them the most and explain to the group why they chose that one.

❑ Form four small groups (a group can be one person). Hand each group one of the four quotes from the "Words of Warning" section on page 9. Have each group (or person) read the quote and think of reasons why someone would say that. After a few minutes, have people report their quotes and their reasons. Ask what other things they'd add to the state of learning in the church from their own personal experiences.

FINDING YOUR WAY

❑ Place a stack of Bibles on the floor and say: **Do something with these Bibles.** Be ready for some bewildered looks and questions. Say nothing more than, "Do something with these Bibles." Observe the group's reactions and let people do "whatever." After a few minutes of confusion, stop and have people pair up to discuss this question:

● **How did you feel when you got my directions?** (For example, people might say, "frustrated," "confused," or "challenged.")

Have pairs report back. Then ask:

● **How is this like learning in the church?** (For example, someone might say, "I knew I was supposed to do something, but I didn't know what," or "We know we're supposed to teach the Bible, but we don't know where to start.")

❑ Tie people's responses into your explanation of why you feel something needs to be done now concerning learning in the church. Paraphrase portions of this chapter or the introduction if you'd like. Tell why knowing the goal is so critical. For instance, if you don't know the goal, it's as frustrating as the activity to "do something with the Bibles."

❑ Next, *do* something with the Bibles. Hand one to each person and assign these verses among the group members: Psalm 19:7; Psalm 119:33-35; John 3:16-17; John 14:6; Colossians 1:28; Colossians 4:2-4; 2 Timothy 3:15-17; James 1:18; and 1 Peter 2:2. Form pairs and have partners explain to each other how their particular passage might speak to learning in the church. Have people report discoveries to the group.

❑ This would be a good place for a brief five- to 10-minute break.

GETTING TO THE GOAL

❑ Now give pairs paper and pencils. Have them list as many purposes of Christian education as they can think of. Encourage them to brainstorm lots of ideas and not pass judgment on any of them at this time.

❑ Call the group together and list on newsprint what they discussed. Nudge people to add to the listing and realize there are many possibilities. Get them all in writing.

❑ Explain that many of the ideas are valuable, but it's important to have a specific, clear direction. To bring the group's goal into focus, pass out green, yellow, and red ¾-inch circle stickers (available from business supply stores). Explain that the colors represent a stoplight.

LEADER TIP

If you can't hunt up ¾-inch circle stickers anywhere, you can always use green, yellow, and red crayons or markers.

- Green means "go"—very important.
- Yellow means "caution"—okay, but not that important right now.
- Red means "stop"—not important for the time being.

Allow each person a certain number of greens, yellows, and reds, depending on the length of your list. For instance, if you have 30 ideas listed, allow five dots of each color per person.

❏ Invite each person to cast his or her "stoplight votes." (This is great fun and allows each person an equal voice and participation in prioritizing the list.)

❏ Stand back and view the list. Ask the group for "aha's" and patterns. What does this list show about the direction for your church's learning goal?

❏ Together, work on a way to say in one simple sentence what your purpose for learning in the church should be. This is hard work, so be an encourager as you work together to complete this sentence: "The goal of learning for (your church's name) is to . . . "

Explain the reason for keeping the goal succinct: It's for future reference and memorability. Too many churches get trapped by a flowery, wordy vision statement that no one can remember, one that nobody ever refers to again. In contrast you want your goal statement to be a "working" statement, one everyone can recite in a simple sentence. It really helps keep it at the forefront if people can easily say it. It's a handy working tool to keep the church on track. Each time a decision needs to be made in education, you can go back and ask, "Does this help us meet our goal?"

WRAPPING UP

❑ Write the goal in big letters for all to see. Say it in unison a few times. (For example, be a cheerleader and ask, "What's our goal?" They respond. Then ask again, "What's our goal?") Celebrate your accomplishment by giving yourselves a hand— maybe even a standing ovation!

❑ Next, decide how you'll get the word out about your goal and your concerns about learning in the church. Ask if anyone would like to continue working on this concern. If so, how?

For example, spark ideas by offering options such as

● a "goal" publicity task force;

● a swat team to study the problem—perhaps this book could be the basis for further explorations; or

● a catalyst group for reviewing what's presently happening at your church and how it could be improved.

❑ Collect names of people and what they'd be willing to do. Ask for names of others to contact for future responsibilities.

❑ Conclude by joining hands for a sentence prayer. Have each person complete this prayer starter:

"Lord, now that we have a clear goal, help us . . . "

3. Follow up with what you decided to do.
After all the effort in your goal-setting meeting, don't let your accomplishments die on the vine. This is just the start of something big. You can change why nobody learns much of anything at church!

GETTING THE GOAL IN FRONT OF PEOPLE

Build awareness of your church's vision. Try these ideas.

● Print it in the church bulletin, preceding each week's calendar of educational offerings.

● Decorate colorful bulletin boards that splash your goal on the walls of your church.

● Display it at the top of each committee's agenda for each meeting.

● Paste stickers with your goal on each teachers manual.

● Create fun buttons that broadcast your goal for leadership, teachers, and parents to wear.

● Incorporate your goal into your church's annual report to remind members of your direction.

● Create long computer-printed banners of your goal to hang in every classroom.

● Place it on a schedule board that lists the church's educational options.

● Put it in your church brochure (if you have one) to let new members learn about your goal.

2 FOCUS ON LEARNING RATHER THAN TEACHING

The preacher spoke for 30 minutes. His content was solid, theologically correct in every detail. He said all the right things, using good grammar and sophisticated vocabulary. He *taught* some great stuff.

But did anybody *learn* any great stuff? The next night at a church potluck the parishioners were asked, "What was the point of the pastor's sermon yesterday?" Only two out of 50 had any idea.

Teaching and learning are not synonymous. Curriculum publishers sell boxcar loads of printed pieces they call teaching materials. Here's an example from a well-known Christian publisher's fifth- and sixth-grade student materials:

Can you turn GUILT into JOY by changing only one or two letters at a time?
GUILT

— — — —
sea bird

— — — —
male bovine

— — —
opposite of sell

— — —
opposite of girl

JOY

Some might call that exercise teaching. But can anyone call it learning? Do those fifth- and sixth-graders now understand how to turn guilt into joy (without first becoming a male bovine)?

Teaching and learning are not synonymous.

Once again, Christian education is not alone. Our public schools have been doing a lot of teaching. But have our kids been doing a lot of learning? The National Assessment of Educational Progress found that math teaching is producing disappointing math learning. For example, only 44 percent of high school graduates could calculate the change they'd receive from $3 after buying two items on a lunch menu.[1]

Albert Shanker, president of the American Federation of Teachers, found that only 12 percent of 17-year-olds were able to arrange six common fractions in order of size, and only 4 percent could figure out a sample bus schedule. He said that only 20 to 25 percent of today's students can learn effectively from traditional methods of teaching.[2]

Yet we continue to use these traditional methods of teaching in the schools and in the church. Why? The word "traditional" probably explains it all. We continue teaching with blind disregard for learning because it's how we were taught. You see, even if we failed to learn the subject matter in school, we did learn the methodology. We all know how school is supposed to look and sound. Teachers hand out banal worksheets and stand in front of students and dispense knowledge.

That, to most of us, is teaching. But it's not learning. Lynn Stoddard, director of the National Alliance for Redesigning Education, writes in his book *Redesigning Education:*

"We must shift from the traditional

role of 'knowledge dispenser' to that of
model, mentor, and organizer of
experiences that help students grow."[3]

A DANGEROUS ASSUMPTION

We've bumped along in the church so long doing our teaching thing that we've rarely stopped to take stock of our effectiveness. We simply assume that if we're teaching, our flock must be learning. It's a dangerous assumption.

We recently stationed ourselves outside of elementary and middle schools in our community. We asked kids pouring out of these schools about their church and Sunday school experience. Happily, most of these kids were church-attenders. But sadly, hardly any could remember even a single thing they learned from any of their church classes.

In a Group Publishing national survey of fifth- and sixth-graders, 54 percent couldn't recall one thing they learned in their church class that same week.

"There is a general assumption that teaching should result in learning and that learning is the consequence of teaching," writes Professor Frank Smith in his book *Insult to Intelligence*. "The problem with this assumption is that the student tends to be blamed for failure to learn. The thought is rarely entertained that teachers might not be teaching what they think they are teaching. A teacher or program may be teaching 'reading skills,' but the student might be learning 'reading is boring' or 'I am a dummy.' "[4]

THE HIDDEN CURRICULUM

In the church, if we may not be teaching what we think we're teaching, what *are* we teaching? Let's look at some possibilities:

WHAT WE THINK WE'RE TEACHING	WHAT THEY MAY BE LEARNING
Big doses of God's Word in a lengthy sermon.	"If God is as boring and tedious as this preacher, count me out."
Clever word puzzles that teach God's eternal truths.	"God and the Bible are confusing and hide the truth from me."
Eloquent prayers that reflect the majesty of God.	"I'll never be able to learn that foreign language God uses."
Students please God by sitting still, being quiet, and listening to the teacher talk.	"Church is where you sit idly while other people take care of the thinking and doing."

What people actually learn in educational settings is often called the "hidden curriculum." Ohio University education professor George Wood says, "When children are reminded day after day, year after year, that the most important thing they can do in school is to sit quietly, obey the teacher, and repeat back verbatim what they have been told, they are learning patterns of thinking and behavior that will stay with them for life. We need look no further than classrooms of passivity to find one of the many sources of civic and intellectual passivity in daily life."[5]

LEARNING GOOD STUFF

Teaching good stuff isn't good enough. We must be certain our people are learning good stuff. How do we do that?

First, we must unlearn how we were taught. We sat quietly in little desks, in sterile classrooms, with a teacher who lectured to us. We filled time with reams of fill-in-the-blank worksheets and tests. We rarely worked together with other students. We memorized the facts we thought the teacher wanted us to know, rarely pursuing what we might want to know.

We must not blindly accept this clichéd picture of the learning environment.

Next, as teachers we must realize that knowing our subject matter isn't good enough. We must know how to enable our students to learn the subject matter and live it. How much time do our Christian colleges and seminaries spend teaching the tiniest nuances of theory and theology, rather than helping their students learn effective methods to generate true learning in their future churches? What good is all our knowledge if it does not affect the lives of the people among whom God has placed us?

The master teacher Jesus gives us some clues about how to help people genuinely learn.

JESUS' LEARNING TECHNIQUES

1. Start with the learner's context. Jesus used objects and story subjects that were familiar to his learners. Boats. Fish. Sheep. Water. Wine. Bread. Fig trees. Seeds. Grain. He started where they were. He knew that effective learning builds upon what the learner already knows.

We can follow Jesus' example. What are the familiar tools of a group of third-graders? Toys! We can use these tools—as Jesus did—to help kids learn from their own context. A Sunday school class filled with the objects kids love presents a fertile learning ground.

What are the familiar symbols for the grown-ups in your adult classes and in your sermon audiences? Car keys, briefcases, aprons, checkbooks, newspapers. Use these icons—as Jesus did—to help your adults learn from their own context. Bring these items into your church as visual learning tools.

Starting with the learner's context emphasizes learning, not teaching.

2. Allow learners to discover truth. Jesus beckoned Peter to walk on the water—to learn about faith (Matthew 14:25-33). Peter discovered a bit of truth through his own experience. Jesus could have simply lectured Peter about faith, but he wanted Peter to *discover.* After Jesus pulled Peter from the water, he asked the disciple, "Why did you doubt?" He could have *told* Peter, but he *asked* instead. Because he wanted Peter to discover.

We can use this same technique—not necessarily walking on water, but discovery learning. People learn best when they discover answers for themselves. In discovery learning the teacher steps away from being the prime dispenser of answers and becomes more of a coach and facilitator.

If we're more interested in *teaching,* we can tell our class how God's power and creativity are present in nature. But if we're more interested in *learning,* we'll take the class outside and let them discover God's handiwork.

With discovery learning, the emphasis is on learning, not teaching.

3. Take advantage of teachable moments. The woman caught in adultery (John 8:1-11). The storm on the lake (Luke 8:22-25). The paralytic in the synagogue (Matthew 12:9-13). Jesus knew when his learners were ripe for learning. He never hesitated to create a lesson out of what happened around him. In contrast to the rote practices of the Pharisees, Jesus knew the difference between teaching and learning. When he observed people engaged in a captivating activity, he knew they were ready to learn. And he took advantage of the opportunity.

In our church settings, we too can take advantage of teachable moments. We can begin by accepting that our learners will learn little if they're uninterested or bored. When they're truly captivated by something, they're already learning. Our job as teachers is to help them wring out the good Christian truths inherent in the present situation.

For example, if freckle-faced Bobby pulls the chair out from under dainty little Sara, you've got your teachable moment. Forget the printed curriculum for that day. Keep the crafts on the shelf. All your learners are focused on this little girl who's just splatted onto the floor. With her wispy Sunday dress flopped over her head, the class prankster has stripped her of her dignity. Now your students are ready to learn. Process the situation with them. Ask how Sara is feeling. Ask the others if they've ever been a victim like Sara. How did they feel? Why do we laugh at another's expense? Will Sara forgive Bobby? Why or why not?

The kids won't forget a session like that. Nor will they forget what they learned.

When seizing teachable moments, the emphasis is on learning, not teaching.

4. Provide learners opportunities to practice what they've learned. Jesus instructed the rich young man, then challenged him to sell all his possessions (Mark 10:17-21). Jesus taught his disciples about betrayal, then gave Peter, Judas, and the others time to practice their loyalty (Matthew 26:31-49). Their failures during practice seared the lesson into their memories.

Few lessons stick without actively putting those lessons to work. You can hear a lecture on riding a bike, but if you don't practice, you'll never ride. You can read a book on gardening, but if you don't practice turning the soil and planting the seeds, you'll never harvest a vegetable. You can unscramble the word "servant" in your church lesson, but if you don't practice serving, you'll never become a servant for Jesus Christ.

If we're teaching—in a class or in a sermon—about telling others how God is working in our lives, we need to let our people practice. Right there. We can ask each person to turn to a partner and tell what God has recently done for him or her. Everybody practices. Right there. That practice will result in genuine learning.

Allowing learners to practice what they've learned puts the emphasis on learning, not teaching.

VERIFY LEARNING

Sadly, most churches today spend more time worrying about teaching than learning. And there's probably a pervasive reason for this. Everyone assumes that the teaching is producing learning. No one bothers to verify that learning is indeed occurring.

Oh, some attempts have been made at verification. Teachers drill and grill their students on Bible memory verses. And teachers look for the answers they want in fill-in-the-blank papers. But these are the tactics of our failed secular schools. They don't really tell us if our students understand the subject matter or have discovered how to apply it to their everyday lives.

If we'd take the time to actually verify our people's learning (or lack thereof), we'd shift our emphasis from teaching to learning in an instant.

If preachers would plant themselves in the church parking lot and interview arriving worshipers about last week's sermon, they'd change their approach to preaching. After attending dozens of churches and hearing hundreds of sermons, no preacher has ever bothered to ask us if he or she caused learning to take place. No one's ever asked us, "What do you remember from last week's sermon? What was the main point? How did it relate to you? Give me an example of how you've lived your life differently as a result of something you heard in my sermon."

The aversion to verification is systemic throughout the church. For years we've heard youth ministers grumble about how poorly their Christian colleges and seminaries prepared them for youth work. And we've asked a number of these institutions how they measure their effectiveness among their alumni. Do they contact their alumni a few years after they've been on the job? Do they ask how well their curriculum prepared their students for real-life ministry? Do they solicit suggestions for improving learning at their institutions? We've found this type of verification to be rare.

Customer satisfaction surveys and toll-free customer response lines are standard fixtures in the business world. Even at the local diner, the server asks, "How was your dinner?" But in the church we avoid soliciting feedback.

Why? A former pastor of ours gave a clue that probably explains a good bit of the problem. When a congregational long-range planning committee suggested administrating a general churchwide questionnaire, the senior pastor nixed the idea. "I don't like surveys," he said. "All they do is give people a chance to complain." We often don't verify because we're afraid of what we'll hear.

But if we care about helping our people become followers of Christ, we must verify that it's happening. We must verify that learning is occurring, not merely that teaching is occurring. The next part of this chapter will give you some tools to help in the learning verification process.

The "DO IT" section that follows offers practical programming ideas to help you share and apply these principles in your church.

DO IT Grapple with the "learning vs. teaching" question. Involve others in unearthing information through the following techniques. Then let teachers discover new ways to approach their role with the training ideas that follow.

UNEARTHING INFORMATION

● **Ask people what they've learned.** Too often we forget to ask the recipients of our educational efforts what they've learned. So here are some ways to gather information on what your children, youth, and adults understand about the Christian faith.

● **Conduct written surveys.** Create a simple confidential questionnaire to hand out during a regular class time or worship service. Or include blank surveys with a regular church mailing, such as the church newsletter, with a date to be returned. Check out the sample questionnaire on pages 48 and 49. Surveys don't even need to be that elaborate. Distribute 3×5 cards to fill out after a sermon, for example. Have people jot "One thing I learned from today's sermon is..." Or "One thing I'll do differently as a result of this lesson is..." And if you really want to take a risk, ask what one thing they remember from last week's sermon!

This same technique works in a classroom. For instance, ask, "What lesson do you remember most?

Why?" or "What have you done this past week as a result of what you've learned?"

● **Do spoken interviews.** This can be powerful if you record them to share with teachers and church leadership. Videos work great, and so do audiocassettes. The interview technique works well with children who can't yet read or write. (Some people don't believe small children can articulate what they've learned. But we disagree. Some youngsters have been the most insightful!)

● **Make informal contacts.** Use this book as a springboard for informal conversations among church members and friends. Check around. Ask people to tell about their church learning experiences. You may be surprised by the feedback once people have been asked to give their honest impressions.

Use the information gathered to verify how your church is actually faring in its educational endeavors. Publish the results. Use the information as a catalyst for committee actions or teacher feedback. You may find you're doing a great job of reaching your learning goal. If not, use it as a call to action.

● **Analyze what you're teaching.** Have teachers brainstorm everything that happens during a typical class time from start to finish; for example, students' first impressions as they arrive, the room arrangement and decor, the lesson's teaching methods (activities, lecture, pencil and paper work, memory drills, snacks).

Create two columns on newsprint. Label the left side "What We Think We're Teaching." Label the right "What They May Be Learning." Carefully, and with an open mind, analyze each segment of class. Imagine what goes through the students' minds and hearts. Then write a plus (+) or minus (-) beside each learning, depending on how positive or negative it could be for the students. Refer to the listings on page 38 earlier in the chapter for ideas.

When the list is finished, discuss: Why was this exercise so difficult to do? What surprised you about the + and - list? What is our church's predominant "hidden curriculum?" What learning areas are strong points? weak points? What changes could you make to move the focus from teaching to learning?

Try this some Sunday in the church parking lot. Ask people what they remember from last week's sermon

MORE INTERVIEW QUESTIONS

● What do you remember from last week's sermon? Sunday school class? youth group? adult Bible class?

● What was the main point?

● How did the lesson relate to you?

● What's an example of how you've lived your life differently because of what you learned from a sermon or class?

● Do you think about God on a daily basis?

● What's been the most relevant teaching the church has given you? Why?

● What one thing would you change about learning in your church?

CONFIDENTIAL QUESTIONNAIRE

We want your input! Please take a few moments to complete this confidential questionnaire. Write only what you remember. Don't refer to the Bible or any other book for help with these answers. If you don't know an answer, just write "I don't know."

When you're finished, place this survey in the provided envelope and seal it. No one will know this is your survey. Please be honest.

Thank you for your help.

1. Think back to the last time you attended Sunday school. What did you learn at that lesson?
2. How would you describe Sunday school and church?
3. What must people do to get to heaven after they die?
4. Who is Jesus?
5. Why did Jesus have to die?
6. What happened to Jesus after his death and burial?
7. What could you do that would make God stop loving you?
8. Who is the Holy Spirit?
9. How would you describe God?
10. In the past 7 days, have you read the Bible while you were alone? ❑ yes ❑ no

11. In the past 7 days, have you prayed by yourself? ❏ yes ❏ no

12. In the past 7 days, has your family prayed together, other than giving thanks for meals? ❏ yes ❏ no

13. In the past 7 days, has your family read the Bible together? ❏ yes ❏ no

14. How often do you talk to your friends about God? ❏ never or rarely ❏ sometimes ❏ often

15. Which of the following best describes your relationship with Jesus Christ? ❏ I don't really have a relationship with Jesus Christ ❏ I'm not sure ❏ I'm committed to Christ

16. Think about what you're taught in classes at church. How often do those lessons shape how you think or act outside of church? ❏ often—every week ❏ sometimes—maybe once or twice a month ❏ rarely—maybe once or twice a year ❏ never—those lessons don't relate to my life

17. Why do you go to classes at church? ❏ I want to ❏ someone makes me go ❏ other _____

Thank you for taking the time to fill out this survey. Please return it to:

or Sunday school class. Or find out right after church, "What was the point of the pastor's sermon?"

It's also helpful to ask people to describe learning in the church. Have them recall the last time they attended Sunday school or some other learning function. What did they learn during that lesson? What do they remember most about church or Sunday school? How are their lives different because of what they learned?

Use the sample questions in the box on page 47. Or adapt the questionnaire on pages 48 and 49.

TRAINING TEACHERS FOR LEARNING

Explore Jesus' style of teaching. Launch an adult Bible class to explore how Jesus taught. Use the following teacher training times that delve into "Jesus' Learning Techniques" found on pages 39 to 42.

TEACHER TRAINING 1:
Start With the Learners' Context

❑ Begin by having teachers each find an object that's "tossable"—something from "their world." For example, a set of car keys, a shoe, a billfold, a hat. Form groups no larger than six. Have group members stand in a circle and hand all the objects to one person in the circle. (How about the person who's been teaching the longest?) Beginning with one object, have that person toss it to someone across the circle. Continue tossing the object across the circle until it returns to the original "tosser." Once the group has established a pattern for tossing (each person always tosses to the same person and receives from the same person), throw in another object. Do this until every object is flying through the air. Things will get a little wild and crazy! After a few minutes, stop the activity and ask:

● **How did you feel during that experience?** (Frustrated; challenged; a sense of teamwork.)

● **How is that like your busy schedules?** (Too many things are going on at once; it helped when we got organized; we needed to all carry some responsibility to make it work.)

● **How did the objects represent things in your life that keep you busy?** (The keys represent how I'm driving my kids everywhere; the shoe stands for running from task to task.)

● **What might Jesus want to tell you about your schedule?** (Slow down; choose only what's most important to do and "toss" the rest; use the support of other people to face the day.)

Dissect the juggling activity you just used to help people get in touch with their schedules. What made the activity interesting? What made it relevant?

Ponder Jesus' teaching style—he always tried to reach his listeners by pointing to their world, what was all around them. Read or paraphrase section 1 from "Jesus' Learning Techniques" on page 39. See how the activity used items from their world to help illustrate a point.

❑ Form four groups and assign each group one of the following age levels: small children, elementary children, youth, and adults. Have the groups each brainstorm a list of what's familiar to each age level's "world." For example, groups might list a stuffed animal, a baseball bat, a Walkman, and a computer. Have groups report their lists to the whole group.

❑ Assign each group one of these Scriptures: Matthew 5–7; Matthew 13; Matthew 18; and Matthew 25. Have groups hunt for examples of how Jesus taught within the context of people's lives, using common objects and stories. Jot them down and report back. Discuss what surprised the teachers about this exercise.

❑ To explore how to strengthen this approach in the classroom, have pairs select a common object from their brainstorming lists. Take time to create a story or activity that teaches a spiritual truth from that object or context. If time allows, have teachers try out their new lesson on the group. If not, at least have them tell what they might do.

❑ Encourage teachers to evaluate their teaching methods. Have them each choose one way they can incorporate the learners' context into their teaching. Return to the pairs from the earlier activity to tell about what they'll commit to doing for future lessons. Close with partners praying for each other.

TEACHER TRAINING 2:
Allow Learners to Discover Truth

GETTING STARTED

❏ Before this training session prepare slips of paper, each with one of these Scripture passages: Mark 1:21-28 (Jesus amazes people by forcing out an evil spirit); Mark 2:1-12 (Jesus heals and forgives a paralyzed man and poses a "Which is easier?" question; Mark 4:35-41 (Jesus calms a storm and some frightened disciples); and Mark 8:14-21 (Jesus warns about false teaching, but the disciples don't get it). For fun, place each Scripture in a colorful plastic egg or roll each Scripture into a scroll and tape or tie it. That'll add to the mood of "discovery." Hide them in your meeting area, one hidden Scripture for every two teachers.

❏ Have the group form pairs. Blindfold one person in each pair and have partners link arms. Explain that the seeing person is the "voice" and the blindfolded person is the "hands." As they search for a "hidden treasure" in the room, they must help each other retrieve the treasure. (Don't tell them what the treasure is.) Let teachers hunt for the verses. When they each find one, the pair must return to you, still linked and one blindfolded until you debrief the experience.

DIGGING IN

❏ When all have found one treasure, join together and discuss:

● **Describe your feelings during the hunt.**

● **Explain how your handicap affected your feelings.**

● **Describe your feelings when you found the treasure.**

● **Tell how this experience is like making discoveries in God's Word.**

● **Explain why discovery learning is so important.**

❏ Now have partners each read their treasure and act it out for the group. (If you repeated the Bible passages to accommodate a larger group, put everyone together who found the same passage.)

SHARING DISCOVERIES

❏ Have teachers perform their stories for the group. After each story, ask:

● **What were the discoveries or "aha's" for the story's characters?**

● **How did Jesus use discovery learning as he taught? What other examples from the Bible can you recall when Jesus used this technique?**

❏ Wrap up by asking teachers to share what their biggest "aha" has been in this training. Conclude with teachers each praying for help on one specific way they will add discovery learning to their classes.

TEACHER TRAINING 3:

Take Advantage of Teachable Moments

GETTING STARTED

❑ Before the meeting, plan for someone to interrupt your meeting. For example, a teacher might stop you in the middle of the session and say, "This is a waste of time!" or someone might fake a fall. The idea is to arrange for a teachable moment while you're explaining teachable moments. Come up with a believable scenario with your interrupter.

❑ Welcome teachers and explain or read section 3 from "Jesus' Learning Techniques" on page 41. Together create a definition for a teachable moment.

DIGGING IN

❑ Form groups of four. Appoint a reader, recorder, encourager, and reporter in each group. Have the readers read the story assigned, the recorders write the people's answers to the questions, the encouragers make sure everyone participates, and the reporters report findings to the whole group. Dole out these passages: Luke 7:36-50 (Jesus' feet get washed with tears and perfume); Luke 8:22-25 (Jesus calms a storm); Luke 9:46-48 (Jesus' followers wondered who was the greatest); Luke 18:35-43 (Jesus makes a blind man see); and Luke 22:14-20 (Jesus uses a meal to remember him by).

❏ Have groups discuss and report back:

● **Describe the setting and situation.**

● **How did Jesus use the situation as a teachable moment?**

● **What do you think the people involved back then were thinking and feeling?**

● **What made the teaching so powerful?**

❏ Sometime during these questions, cue your "plant" to disrupt the discussion. Carry on your interruption until you see people have become duly intrigued. "Stop the camera" and ask how people felt during the interruption; compare those feelings to what happens with real teachable moments in the classroom.

REACHING OUT

❏ Next, assign each group a category of unexpected events: in the classroom, in the church, in the community, at school, in the workplace, at home, and in the world. Allow time for brainstorming teachable moments from those settings. Examples might include a discipline problem, someone teasing someone else, a suicide, someone getting laid off from work, someone reprimanding the youth group for messing up the church kitchen, or someone not making the team.

❏ Have groups exchange ideas on strengthening teaching by incorporating what's happening in people's lives. Create a list of ideas on newsprint. When the list is finished, place it on the floor. Have teachers form a circle around it. One by one, have teachers rip a small piece from the list while they pray for the ability to incorporate teachable moments in the classroom. Call it a "tear prayer."

TEACHER TRAINING 4:

Provide Learners Opportunities to Practice What They've Learned

GETTING STARTED

❏ Use this teacher training session to show how teachers can help students put faith into action right away. Open with prayer and read John 1:1-5. Talk about how God's Word needs to come to life and be put into action through Jesus Christ. That's the essence of teaching—changing lives and helping people live the gospel. The rest of the training will show how you can read and practice Scripture right in class.

TRYING IT OUT

❏ Have a volunteer read Philippians 2:4. Practice those words. Have teachers turn to a partner and share:

● **What's your name and what's your favorite childhood memory?**

● **What's the greatest joy in your life right now?**

● **What's your greatest burden right now?**

● **How can your partner give you support right now?**

Reread the verse and discuss other ways to put

those words into action in a classroom.

❏ Have a volunteer read 2 Corinthians 4:5. We always tell students to tell others about Jesus and share their faith. But how do we do that? Have people turn to their partners again and tell each other how God has worked in their lives.

Light a candle and read 2 Corinthians 4:5-6. Thank people for letting their light shine as teachers.

❏ Read Ephesians 1:15-20. Divide into prayer teams. Then have teams divide the church building into sections; for example, the education rooms, the sanctuary, the kitchen, the nursery, and the office. Assign teams two or more of the areas to go to and pray for the people who help "make it happen" there and for the people served there. Set a time for everyone to return. Share what it felt like to actually pray for your church.

❏ Read Philippians 2:5-7. Explain that they'll get a chance to become like servants. Pass out spray bottles of window cleaner and rags. Send teams of teachers outside into the parking lot. Have them wash as many windshields as they can in 10 minutes, then return. Observe how teachers react. Do they grumble? see it as a fun challenge? complain that they'll get dirty or cold? After people return, debrief the experience.

❏ Now it's time for goal-setting. Discuss what a difference acting on God's Word makes. What kinds of things can they do in the classroom to allow participants to practice their faith? Have teachers plan specific ways to allow "practice" sessions in class.

Have someone read Philippians 3:12-14. Have each teacher write and tell a goal—a commitment that helps learners practice their faith.

CELEBRATING

❏ In closing, give thanks to God. Form six groups (a group can be one person). Assign each group to read one of these passages, then decide how they'll involve the rest of the group in thanksgiving: Psalm 92:1-2; Psalm 92:3; Psalm 92:4-5; Psalm 92:7-8; Psalm 92:12-14; and Psalm 92:15. Allow a few minutes for planning. Then have each group give thanks by involving the group in what their passage inspired.

Close with a favorite song of praise and thanksgiving.

3 CONCENTRATE ON THE ESSENTIALS

The student pilot gripped the airplane's controls as the ground seemed to rocket toward him. The flight instructor at his side nonchalantly rattled on about the altitude's effect on air temperature. "Notice how the temperature rises approximately 3.5 degrees with every 1,000 feet we drop," he said.

The student was terrified. He didn't want to hear about temperature theories. He wanted to know how to land the airplane!

The instructor was very knowledgeable. But he sometimes forgot that his student didn't yet know the basics of flight. The teacher was overeager to move on to more interesting aspects of flying.

Sometimes we're tempted to do the same in our churches. We become preoccupied with so many things to teach that we overlook the essentials of the faith. We forget to teach our learners how to land the plane.

Do they know the essentials? Let's look at some statistics:

● A Group Publishing survey of churchgoing fifth- and sixth-graders found that 72 percent do not know the meaning of baptism. And 40 percent do not understand the meaning of Jesus' death. Only nine percent know who the Holy Spirit is. And only 13 percent can name Jesus' two great commandments.[1]

● Sixty-two percent of churchgoing adults believe that

Christians, Muslims, Buddhists, and others all pray to the same God, according to the Barna Research Group.[2]

● A Search Institute study found that 46 percent of churchgoing teenagers and 67 percent of churchgoing adults have trouble understanding salvation as a gift instead of something earned.[3]

Too many people in our churches today do not understand the most basic elements of the Christian faith. And we as educators must accept a large share of the responsibility for that. Only when we stop looking outside ourselves will we begin to make learning effective in the church. Only then will our people understand—and live—the essentials of our faith.

Only 49 percent of churchgoing youth say their churches provide good teaching on applying their faith to everyday decisions.[4] We all must accept responsibility for that mediocre statistic. We must look inward when only 28 percent of adults strongly agree that the Christian churches in their area are relevant to the way people live these days.[5]

Somehow, we've designed an educational process that allows our learners to miss the obvious. How could that happen? Where have we derailed? Well, we've spotted three root problems:

1. We assume knowledge and understanding where none exists.

2. We've bought into the "more is better" approach to teaching.

3. We fail to tell our people what's most important.

Let's look at each of these areas.

ASSUME NOTHING

Sometimes the basics of the faith seem so elementary to us. As educators we become eager to move on to more interesting stuff. It's like we've been anesthetized to the simple gospel message. We're numbed into believing that our people know the basics when they do not.

Salvation, most would agree, is a pretty basic and essential concept of our faith. But it's dangerous to assume all our kids and adults understand salvation.

Our study of churchgoing fifth- and sixth-graders revealed some pretty interesting plans for eternal life. One fifth-grade girl said, "A person gets to heaven by having a good personality and following God's rules." When we asked what God's rules were, she didn't know.

Sixty-one percent of fifth- and sixth-grade Sunday school students are unsure of their relationship with Jesus Christ.[6]

We recently conducted a lock-in for the junior high kids at our church. The theme was forgiveness. We began by asking the kids to list some common sins. A few kids volunteered some possibilities. But their peers argued loudly that those sins weren't necessarily sins. "It depends!" they shouted. We were dealing with basic Ten Commandments stuff here. But the kids wouldn't allow those items on the sin list.

That part of our lesson took a lot longer than we anticipated. We made the mistake of assuming the presence of some basic beliefs. We were wrong.

Later in the evening we saw the life consequences of our kids' skewed beliefs. They had agreed upon a set of rules for the overnighter. One of the rules stated that no one was allowed to venture beyond one wing of the building. We used paper streamers to mark the boundary at the end of the hall. Well, it wasn't an hour after the kids signed the conduct covenant that several of them tore through the streamers and ran into the other part of the church.

We called everybody together to discuss the infraction. Everyone, including the culprits, agreed the boundary had been violated. We asked, "What should we do about this violation of the rules that everyone agreed to?" Their response: "Move the boundary." Suddenly their earlier problem identifying any real sins became frighteningly relevant. These kids' ignorance of God's essentials shapes their everyday thinking and decision making.

We can't assume kids know the essentials. Neither can we assume adults know the essentials. After observing the low attendance at our own church's Sunday morning adult classes, we talked with some of the folks playing hooky in the halls. "Why aren't you in the pastor's class right now?" we asked. Some common responses: "They lose me in that class." "I'm afraid if I open my mouth in there I'll make a fool of myself." "The last time I went the pastor asked me to read something from the Bible, and I didn't know where to find that book in the Bible. I felt like an idiot."

It's fine to offer separate advanced studies for those who've mastered the essentials. But we must always emphasize the basics for the majority. We've seen some churches offer adult classes on environmentalism, governmental affairs, and denominational history but neglect topics like "Introduction to Jesus," "Bible Basics," and "Applying Your Faith on the Job."

Our kids and adults exhibit biblical illiteracy and a shallow faith because we've assumed they know, understand, and apply more than they do.

LESS IS MORE

We make another big teaching blunder when we think more is better. We try to cram so much into our people's noggins that they haven't a clue what's essential and what isn't. In fact, when we throw them so many balls to juggle, they wind up dropping them all.

Our intentions are good. We have so much to share. Our kids and adults have so much to learn. Time is so short. We want our people to have it all. We're afraid they'll go away empty-handed or disappointed if we don't pepper them with everything we know on the subject.

Once again, we in the church have made the same mistake our nation's schools have made. Many well-intentioned observers cry that our kids need "more"—more drilling, more homework, more standardized tests. All of this is based on the assumption that spraying our kids with more information will result in more learning. But there's no evidence this is true. Ohio University education professor George Wood says, "Exposure does not equal learning. And exposure certainly does not equal retention. By having students cover even more material it virtually assures that nothing will be covered in depth. Students may become good Trivial Pursuit players, but they will be lousy citizens and neighbors."[7]

It's no secret that Japanese students perform better and learn more than American students. One explanation for this may lie in Japan's understanding of "less is more." In America you might find second-graders spending 30 minutes slogging through two or three pages of arithmetic problems. But in Japan the students would spend the same amount of time examining just a couple of problems in depth, picking apart the reasoning process necessary to solve them.[8]

In one Japanese first-grade reading class, American observers saw an entire 40-minute period spent on just 29 words describing a single episode from a 252-word story. That class typically covers just two stories a month.[9]

> ## "Less is more.
> ## Thoroughness counts more
> ## than coverage."
>
> *—Ted Sizer, chairman of the*
> *Coalition of Essential Schools*

Some American schools are realizing that less is more. Fourth-grade teacher Mick Cummings at Amesville (Ohio) Elementary School says, "I never worry about covering everything in the book . . . racing through a textbook is not the way kids learn. What is important is that we do a few things very well and that the kids really get into it and take charge. We learn how to learn, how to find out, what the general concepts are. The children score just as well or better on the standardized tests when we do it this way, but that's not the point. The point is that they are taking control of what they learn."[10] And they'll likely learn stuff that will stick with them for life.

NOT ENOUGH BIBLE?

At Group Publishing we use a "one lesson, one point" approach in the children's Bible curriculum we create. The kids often spend an entire hour delving into one short Bible passage. And our loudest critics cry, "There's not enough Bible!" They believe if kids would just trudge through umpteen verses per hour, then they'd really learn.

But coverage does not equal understanding. We must remember the goal. Is the goal to spray as much Bible at our students as possible? Or is the goal to help them understand and apply biblical truths to their lives?

Jesus never rushed his learners. He never attempted to pump in more than could be consumed. He never practiced the "more is better" approach. In fact, he said,

"I have many more things to say to you, but they are too much for you now."

—John 16:12

Many modern-day church folk ignore Jesus' approach. They view Bible study and Bible knowledge as spiritual measuring sticks. They judge a person's faith on the number of chapters consumed per week or the number of verses memorized. They purr when their students can generously cite historical details from the books of Habakkuk or Nahum. But they've missed the point. Did God ever intend that the Bible itself become an object of worship? Is knowledge of Bible facts our final goal? It's time to remember the goal. Are we trying to qualify our students for the Bible version of *Jeopardy?* Or are we trying to draw people closer to God and affect the way they live their lives?

We don't increase learning by stuffing in more information than a finite attention span can digest. Cramming too much into one session is like running a long movie on fast forward. You may get through the whole thing in a short time, but all impact is lost. And no one takes home even one essential Bible truth. Our time with our students is too precious, too scarce, to squander it in fast-forward mode.

Many church teachers believe their goal is to accomplish everything in a printed curriculum's agenda for a given lesson. So they speed through the lesson, trampling student interest and inquiry along the way. No one's ever told them that *learning* something is more important than *covering* everything.

If—each time we gather with our learners—we can help them learn one single essential point, we're wildly successful. You see, communicating *anything* that people can retain and act upon is hard to do. Trying to accomplish multiple profound learnings in an hour or a half-hour is a trip through Fantasyland.

Again, the law of the farm applies. Cramming too many seeds into a space doesn't create a bumper crop. Rather, plant your seeds in such a way that each has room to germinate, breathe, and grow. Pull out the nearby sprouts that are too close and let the essential plant flourish. And you'll reap a good harvest.

Less is more.

SAY WHAT'S IMPORTANT

Another reason our learners don't know the essentials is that we simply fail to tell them what really is essential.

Kids and adults today live in a fast-paced, confusing world. They're bombarded with new information to the point of overdose. We simply don't have the time to teach them everything. They don't have the time to learn everything. One estimate put the average time a faithful Sunday school attender spends in education time (after subtracting time for taking attendance, getting organized, etc.) at 17 hours per year.

We simply have no time to waste. And it's unfair and unwise to splatter our learners with information, then fail to tell them what's really essential.

Jesus let the Pharisees know which commandments were most important (Matthew 22:34-40). Why don't we tell our learners what's most important for them to learn? Well, once again we may have learned some bad habits from the schools we all attended.

The whole system of checking student competency in our schools taught us to obscure the truly important. How many tests quizzed you on trivia that you no longer remember? Why? They were easy to grade. Educator Dr. Arthur Costa says, "What was educationally significant and hard to measure has been replaced by what is educationally insignificant and easy to measure. So now we measure how well we've taught what isn't worth learning!"[11]

We all learned another negative lesson in school. During our school years we sat through hundreds of long-winded lessons. How often did you hear a student ask, "Out of all this stuff, what's important for us to remember?"

And what did the teacher say? "All of it."

Your teacher was hoping that you'd swallow, digest, and forever remember everything he or she said, everything written on the chalkboard, and everything in the textbook. So you spent your time poring over mountains of unimportant trivia, fearing that it might show up on the exam. What a waste!

Bruce Wilkinson of Walk Through the Bible Ministries believes it's the teacher's job to help students sift through all the "stuff" and say, "Now this is really important!" When Wilkinson was a college professor he got in trouble with school officials because his students scored higher than other classes on their tests. But that's because he told them what was important for them to know.

Does your church have a list of essentials that you believe all your members absolutely, positively need to know? Do you have it broken down by age level? Do you frequently share your list with your learners? And do you lavish learning time on what's absolutely essential? Learners perceive something's value by how much time it receives.

Our people don't know the essentials because we don't bother to tell them what the essentials are.

The plane is screaming toward the ground. The dials are spinning in our students' cockpits. Right now we need to help them learn the most important thing—how to land the plane. We must concentrate on the essentials.

The "DO IT" section that follows offers practical programming ideas to help you share and apply these principles in your church.

DO IT

In the quest for improved learning, it's vital to know what's essential to teach. We all may agree on basic Christian beliefs, yet every church chooses to emphasize certain beliefs. The trouble is, when we clutter the basics with nonessentials, we hamper people's learning. To clarify what people need to learn, check out assumptions and gather information. Then help teachers zero in on those main points. These ideas will help you do that.

PINPOINTING YOUR CHURCH'S ESSENTIALS

1. Make no assumptions. Start here. Find out people's understanding of the Christian faith. Gather information during Bible classes, sermons, informal gatherings, and through mail surveys. Ask people to anonymously write their answers to questions such as these:

● When it comes to the Christian faith, I wish I knew more about...

● When it comes to our church's teachings, I wish I knew more about...

● When it comes to the Bible, I wish I knew more about...

● Why do we do...at church?

● Why don't we do...at church?

● I've always wondered why God...

● In my daily life, I don't understand how God fits into...

● A question about Jesus I've always wanted to ask is . . .

● Something I don't understand about the Holy Spirit is . . .

● Learning in our church would be more relevant to me if it dealt with . . .

Collect the answers and compile a list of ideas. Address them in learning settings such as Sunday school, Bible classes, sermons, and seminars.

2. Check out your assumptions. Too often we think people already know what we know. To challenge your assumptions, make a list of five to 10 things you're absolutely sure people in your class or congregation know. To jump-start your thinking, include statements such as "God loves me," "I believe in Jesus as my personal Lord and Savior," "God forgives all my sins," and "When I die I'll go to heaven."

Hand out paper and pencils and have people number their papers to match the number of statements you've devised. Read each statement and its number while people anonymously respond to each by using these symbols:

● Jot an exclamation point (!) if they're absolutely sure.

● Jot a period (.) if they're kind of sure.

● Jot a question mark (?) if they're not sure.

Tabulate the results and use the information in planning future learning opportunities.

3. Identify what's important to learn in your church. Create a list of faith essentials—the basics. Have people rank them according to importance, or mark the top five for learning the basics.

For example, here are 12 possibilities (by no means exhaustive, just a start):

___God	___Sin
___The Bible	___The church
___Jesus	___Prayer
___The Holy Spirit	___Witnessing
___Creation	___Service and outreach
___Human nature	___Eternity

Here's another approach to an essentials list. Add your own:

___ God Almighty

___ God, creator, maker of heaven and earth

___ Jesus Christ

___ Jesus' birth

___ Jesus' life and ministry

___ Jesus' suffering and death

___ Heaven and hell

___ Jesus' resurrection

___ Judgment, the last days

___ Holy Spirit

___ The church

___ Communion of Saints

___ Forgiveness of sins

___ Salvation

___ Eternal life

___ Your church's sacraments

Or look at how your church is organized. List all the boards and committees (such as worship, service, stewardship, fellowship, outreach, evangelism, education, social ministry). Does each reflect an essential to the Christian faith? Have a group analyze what your church stands for and how it's mobilized for action.

4. Who learns what when? Once you've

selected what essentials to emphasize, create a grid for each age level—children, youth, and adults. Map out which essential items you want people to learn at each age level. Some items may appear in the grid more than once.

Implement a way to assure each age level covers what you feel are the essentials. Use your list as a tool for evaluating curriculum. Publish it for teachers and parents to see. Refer to it when planning. And re-evaluate it every few years.

5. Retrain teachers. Help teachers feel comfortable with the idea that they need not complete every lesson in the teachers manual to be successful. Explain why "less is more" when it comes to teaching biblical truths. Have teachers read the "Less Is More" and "Not Enough Bible?" sections starting on page 65. Form trios to discuss the following questions (and report to the whole group later):

● **What's an example of when you applied the "less is more" concept to something you learned?**

● **How do you measure success in the classroom?**

● **Are you compelled to rush through every activity in the teachers guide? Why or why not?**

● **Why do some people find "less is more" a difficult concept to buy into?**

● **How will you know the difference between taking time to understand a point and dragging out a lesson?**

● **What are the benefits of concentrating**

time on *understanding?* What are the draw-backs?

Together brainstorm one important point to teach. Then in groups no larger than four, come up with ways to drive home that point using a variety of methods (for example, drama, music, art, rhythm, puppets, storytelling, and service projects).

Invite teachers to share their ideas. Form prayer partners to provide support and encouragement to concentrate on "less is more" in their classes.

4 EMPHASIZE UNDERSTAND-ING OVER ROTE MEMORIZATION

The 9-year-old boy stands before his Sunday school class rubbing his forehead, hoping the massage will resurrect the words. The other students fidget nervously, knowing they're next to stand before the scowling teacher.

Mrs. Proonquist squints over the top of her glasses. "You've had a week to work on this, Robert. I want to hear Titus 2:13 and 14."

Robert begins: "Looking for that blessed hope, God... umm... looking for that peculiar person, he might quit and purify the works."

"That's not it, young man. No badge for you. Priscilla, I trust you're better than little Robert here," says Mrs. Proonquist.

"Yes, ma'am," Priscilla says, bounding to her feet. "Looking for that blessed hope, and the glorious appearing of the great God and Savior Jesus Christ; Who gave himself for us, that he might redeem us from all iniquity, and purify unto himself a peculiar people, zealous of good works. Titus 2:13 and 14."

"Thank you, Priscilla, you are one of the Lord's peculiar people," says Mrs. Proonquist as she pins a peculiar-looking badge to the little girl's dress. Priscilla beams as she glances at Robert and the other badgeless students.

Does Priscilla understand the meaning of that passage she so exactly repeated from the King James Version? Will she remember those words a month from now? What did Robert actually learn from this exercise? What's the net long-term result from this investment of class time?

A CURIOUS PROMINENCE

Children's rote memorization of Scripture has taken on a curious prominence in the church. It's another of those hand-me-down goals that few ever stop to analyze.

Memory verses are incorporated into most publishers' weekly lesson plans for children. Many teachers wouldn't consider starting or ending their lessons without a memory drill. Their sole purpose for bringing candy or other refreshments is to reward those kids who're able to repeat their Bible verses. And the memory award-chart often occupies the celebrated place of prominence in many classrooms.

We once asked a group of teachers, "Would you consider doing a lesson that did not contain a memory drill?" One of the teachers said, "Of course not. Why else are we here?"

The practice of children's memory work has itself become sacred, religious. It's been done for so long that no one dares to question its validity or its price.

But, being the adventuresome authors we are, we'd like to dare you to think about this old habit of rote memory work. Does it accomplish what we hope it does? Is it worth the time? Is there a better way?

IS ROTE WRONG
IN THE SCHOOLS?

We grown-ups experienced years of school that included large doses of rote memorization. That regimen defined how we now view education. We've been programmed. And decades of ritual have defined how today's school teachers and administrators mold schools for contemporary children. As a result, millions of kids are compelled to memorize historical dates and names, multiplication tables, and chunks of literature.

Short-term memory skills are the prized factor in today's schoolwork and tests. The typical examination relies on factoid recall—multiple choice, fill-in-the-blanks, and other easy-to-grade devices. "Successful" students, those who've cracked the system, know how to cram. They've learned that the law of the farm does not apply to schoolwork. Cramming works. The reward (grades) goes to those who can temporarily recall certain words and numbers.

"It's testing for the TV generation—superficial and passive," says Linda Darling-Hammond, director of education for the RAND Corporation.[1] Her company and thousands more worry about the quality of education that's reflected in the employees now applying for work. Many corporations have resorted to costly training programs that equip workers with simple skills they should have learned in school. American businesses spend more than $25 billion each year on remedial education for their employees—virtually all of whom attended public schools.[2]

Now, finally, many education experts are scrutinizing and questioning the age-old emphasis on rote memorization. Some of their observations:

"When children must resort to memorizing tricks to pass tests (on material they
don't understand), they soon forget."

—Jane Healy, Endangered Minds [3]

"Much of the learning in traditional systems of imposed instruction is for the
purpose of passing the next test.
Information is put into the brain's 'closed
file' as soon as the test is over because it
has already served its purpose."

*—Lynn Stoddard, Redesigning
Education [4]*

"Rather than believing that children
can be active participants in the con-
struction of their own knowledge,
many textbook writers offer curricula
that depend more on memorization
than on understanding."

*—Harold Stevenson and James
Stigler, The Learning Gap [5]*

"Rote memorization is the worst strategy
for trying to learn anything we do not
understand, including poetry, multiplication tables, and historical dates. Learning

**by rote is the hardest and most pointless
way to learn. Students who use memorized formulas without understanding
commit monumental mistakes without
suspecting their errors."**

—*Frank Smith, Insult to Intelligence* [6]

Some of America's most effective schools are now
placing more emphasis on understanding than on rote
memorization. Their students are learning more and
putting their knowledge to work in real life.

WORKING FOR GRACE

Devotees of Scripture memory programs strongly
defend spending significant time in this activity. They often
cite examples in their own lives when they've recalled
memorized Scripture at crucial times. Remembering good
stuff is a good thing. But how is that memory formed? And
what priority does understanding receive?

No Christian educator would argue against the power
of God's Word. But some would debate how God's
Word is handled by God's people.

Many teachers seem far more interested in seeing
children parrot a Bible verse than understand it. There
seems to be a belief that memorizing something that's
not understood will somehow magically work wonders.
So, significant amounts of time that could be spent on
understanding God's Word are instead spent teaching
children verbiage that seems foreign and confusing.

Julie, our next-door neighbor, sent her two children

to the neighborhood church's vacation Bible school. The first day her 8-year-old boy returned home in tears. He felt like an outcast amidst the other kids who proudly wore their memory ribbons. "Some kids looked like birds they were so covered with ribbons," Julie said.

"The whole program revolved around the memory work," she said. "One girl there could recite 156 verses in a row." Julie's kids tried at first to conform. They really wanted the pretty blue ribbon that was imprinted with "SAVED BY JESUS: 'For by grace are ye saved through faith; and that not of yourselves; it is the gift of God.' Ephesians 2:8." The kids worked into the night drilling each other on the verse that appeared on the ribbon. On their next visit to the church, they missed a word or two. The teacher told them if they wanted that pretty blue "grace ribbon" they'd have to work harder. She never caught the contradiction—the hidden curriculum—of working for grace.

The kids dropped out. "They don't want to ever return," Julie said. "And now they don't remember anything they were drilled on. The teachers never spent any time helping the kids understand the verses. It was a waste of time and turned the kids off to that church."

Sadly, that family's story is not an isolated one.

Steve, an editor we know, remembers a church children's program he attended as a 10-year-old. "I remember the pressure to memorize," he said. "I felt grilled. It seemed like I was always behind." He dropped out after a few months. "Later, every time we drove past that church, I felt negative. I didn't want to get near it."

Jennifer, another adult friend, remembers a similar experience from her childhood. "I went to this church with a friend. Everything was so structured—I felt inadequate.

Since I was a newcomer, I didn't know the last memory verse. So they separated me from my friend—who knew the verse. I went once and never went back," she said.

Another friend, Brenda, retains bad memories from a camp she attended as a 20-year-old. She and three other young adults were assigned a section of Philippians to memorize. They worked on it for a week, then recited their piece for their leader. Brenda missed two words. She and the rest of her group were denied their prize—a camp T-shirt. What she remembers is crying. What she doesn't remember is the passage from Philippians.

Of course many stories could be cited where Scripture memory programs have produced positive results. However, most school-age children we've interviewed do not have positive feelings toward church memory work. For most it's drudgery.

But proponents say, "Kids don't like to brush their teeth, either. But we make them do it because it's good for them. They'll thank us later." Is rote memorization like dental hygiene? Let's dig a little deeper.

WHY ROTE MEMORIZATION IS STRESSED

Scripture memory advocates cite several reasons why the church should pursue memorization regimens. Let's look at some common arguments.

l. The Bible told me so. A frequently mentioned verse is Psalm 119:11. It reads (in the NIV):

> **"I have hidden your word in my heart
> that I might not sin against you."**

This verse is helpful because it supplies an immediate reason for its call to action. David hid the word in his heart so he wouldn't sin. Preventing sin was the goal. What does "hidden your word in my heart" mean? To memorize? To understand? Which is more important for preventing sin: word-for-word memorization or cognitive understanding? Later verses shed some light. Verse 27: "Let me *understand* the teaching of your precepts; then I will meditate on your wonders." Verse 125: "I am your servant; give me discernment that I may *understand* your statutes." Understanding promotes obedience.

And what is the "word"? The book of John provides a most powerful definition:

"In the beginning was the Word, and the Word was with God, and the Word was God. The Word became flesh and made his dwelling among us."

—John 1:1, 14, NIV

Now reread Psalm 119:11 with this definition of "word." How much better will we obey God if we hide the living Christ in our hearts?

A parrot in a pet shop can memorize and recite John 3:16. But only God's human children can know and understand Jesus—can hide him in their hearts.

Beyond proof-texting, the best illustration of Scripture memorization can be found in the life and teachings of Jesus. He quoted Scripture from memory. He used Scripture passages in his teaching. This indicates to us that Scripture memory has value. We can learn several things from Jesus' use of Scripture:

● He always used Scripture to help his learners understand, to illuminate a present situation or teaching. He didn't recite Scripture just to recite Scripture. His goal was understanding.

● He orally shared Scriptures as relevant truths for his listeners, many of whom were illiterate or unfamiliar with the Scriptures. He wanted his people to understand God's Word.

● As a teacher he knew the Scriptures, but he never engaged his students in memory drills. Instead he used his precious time to make people think—and to understand the Word of God.

2. Prepare for emergencies. Stalwarts often promote memorized Scripture as a handy tool when a Bible is unavailable. One Scripture memory guide says, "A man in the army must know the M-16 well enough to be able to tear it down and assemble it blindfolded in the dark in a short amount of time. We should long to know God and his Word far more than a man must know a rifle."

Using this illustration, is the soldier able to assemble the rifle because he knows it and understands it or because he can recite the owners manual word for word?

Until fairly recently, teachers told students about the prospect of Communists breaking into their homes and snatching all the Bibles. When that happens, they reasoned, only the Scriptures inscribed in the faithfuls' memories would survive. Memorization was their only hope. The end of the Cold War deflated many teachers' favorite motivational tool.

However, aside from the melodramatic scenarios, recalling a bit of God's Word can indeed bring comfort and direction in a time of need.

3. Gauge students' progress. Many teachers are

attracted to memorization drills in order to assess children's learning. Spiritual growth is a tough thing to measure. Rote memory is simple to measure. Just listen to the little ones as you'd listen to a trained parrot. When a parrot or a child recites a memory piece, the teacher feels good.

One well-known youth speaker travels about the country chastising young people because he believes they don't measure up. Before he reveals his line of thinking, he urges his audiences to sing familiar commercial jingles. "I wish I were an Oscar Mayer wiener." The kids join in on a long litany of jingles and theme songs. Then he zings them: "You know the words of the world, but not the word of the Lord!" Memorized words and rhymes are his measuring sticks.

The more perceptive kids often corner him after his harangues and share not only their understanding of God's Word, but sing to him the jingles of their faith. They know many more Christian songs than he does.

Recitation of Bible verses is an unreliable gauge of a person's faith. Rote memory is easier for some than others. It's particularly frustrating for those whose minds don't work that way. Word-for-word memorization is a lower-order thinking skill. It is not a spiritual dipstick. Many people with a deep and mature Christian faith cannot readily memorize literary matter word for word. But they understand and act upon God's Word in mighty ways.

WHEN ROTE RUNS AWRY

The defenders of rote memorization drills can and do remind us of the payoff of their programs. But for every payoff there's a price. And here is the real heart and soul of the matter. Can we afford the price for the results attained?

So what is the price of submitting our children to weekly or daily Scripture memorization drills? Let's browse some price tags.

● **Time**—We know that our time with kids in the church is extremely limited. We learned in the last chapter that the typical Sunday school child spends just 17 hours per year in Bible instruction. We do not have the luxury of teaching everything we'd like. Even the best teachers, with the best students, with the best materials, and with the best environment cannot cover everything that really ought to be covered.

So we must make choices.

What will we do with our limited and nonreplenishable resource called time? If we have a choice (and we do) between helping our kids understand and apply God's Word or having them memorize a block of verses, which will better accomplish our overall goal?

"We can do both," you say. Maybe you can. But research shows that our churched children are woefully undernourished when it comes to understanding God's Word.

Is the price—the time we take away from understanding God's Word—worth the payoff?

● **Repellent**—Many teachers beam with pride when

their students arrive with their Bible verses memorized. Those "good" kids get affirmed and often rewarded with candy or stickers. But what about the other kids—those who have trouble with rote memorization or simply disdain the pressure?

As we've seen, they often drop out. Many kids—who otherwise would have learned about God—simply leave and never return. Some never get near a church again.

You see, the ability to memorize words in a certain order is a gift. For some people, it comes quite naturally. It's easy. But for others, word-for-word memorization is a painful, nearly impossible task. Their brains simply aren't wired to work that way.

This is crucial for teachers (and parents) to understand. Teachers tend to teach how they best learn. So teachers who find word-for-word memorization quite easy tend to emphasize that regimen to their students. Those teachers may have little patience for students who seem to struggle with rote memorization. The attitude is: "If I memorized all these verses when I was a child, so can my students do it now."

Some kids today can readily memorize. But many, many cannot. Forcing all kids to learn as their teacher did 20 years ago can do more harm than good.

Yes, we can cite examples of adults who still remember those Sunday school verses from 20 years ago. But are those isolated examples worth the legions of children who were turned off? Can we afford the price?

● **Confusion**—When we emphasize rote memorization over understanding we invite misunderstanding. Many kids rattle off their weekly memory pieces and don't have a clue what they're saying. Others pick up a word here and there and make dangerous assumptions.

A fifth-grade boy we interviewed interpreted his latest memory verse this way: "It's like if you steal or something, you're supposed to cut off your hand." Another Bible-quoting boy in our area did just that several years ago.

Memorizing words without understanding can be dangerous. Mindless memorization leads some people to commit serious mistakes without ever questioning their ways.

Unfortunately this problem is exacerbated by the use of hard-to-understand Bible translations. And it seems that Bible memory's staunchest proponents insist on using the King James Version. Why? "It's conservative," they say. The fact that it's old both in years and style does not make it conservative. Today's conservative Bible translators are no less conservative than King James' translators. They are more learned and accurate in their translating, however.

What's the purpose of insisting that our children memorize lines from the King James Version? If knowing and loving God is our goal, how can we justify deliberately confusing our children? Here's a sample verse from the King James Version—2 Kings 9:8: "For the whole house of Ahab shall perish: and I will cut off from Ahab him that pisseth against the wall, and him that is shut up and left in Israel." That's what it says. Look it up in the KJV.

Is this helpful to our kids? Do you suppose that's the language God wants our kids memorizing?

Memorization without understanding breeds confusion. Can we afford that price?

● **Hidden curriculum**—We discussed in chapter 2 the

difference between teaching and learning. Sometimes what people learn is not at all what we think we're teaching. They learn other subtle stuff called the "hidden curriculum." What's the hidden curriculum with memorization drills?

The importance teachers place on over-and-over repetition of phrases can send a dangerous message. Students can equate Christianity to religions such as Hinduism that attach mystical powers to mantras.

Students may also learn that being a parrot is more important than being a doer of God's Word. The amount of time and emphasis teachers devote to any behavior communicates that behavior's implied value. Students may infer that God's purpose for giving us his Word was to hear us parrot it back at him rather than to live it.

And, what might children learn when they receive candy or trinkets for memorizing a verse? The Bible is not so much a blueprint for our lives but a book of coupons for instant gratification.

Also, the more savvy children notice that Scripture memorization is something imposed upon children but not adults. The hidden message: God's Word is something you grow out of.

Of course not all children are imprinted with these hidden agendas. But some are. Can we afford the price of these possible hidden learnings?

UNDERSTANDING BEFORE MEMORY

Bible memory has a place. Our concern arises when teachers place memorization work before understanding.

Understanding is the key. The Bible itself is God's tool

to help us understand him and his desires for us. A Bible translation is someone's *understanding* of the original Hebrew and Greek. If we truly believe word-for-word rote memorization somehow takes precedence over understanding, why not memorize the Hebrew and Greek? Why trust anybody's *understanding* of the early manuscripts?

The translators realized that understanding was more important than foreign symbols on a page. That's why they translated!

The job of translating God's eternal and unchanging Word goes on today. And the translators reside in your church and ours. They are the teachers, the youth leaders, the pastors, the parents. The teacher's role, the parent's role, is to translate God's Word so the people will understand.

Understanding is the key. And if our people first understand God's Word, they're far more likely to remember his Word.

"Knowledge acquired under compulsion obtains no hold on the mind."

—Plato

Think for a moment about the information you currently hold in your memory bank. Phone numbers, addresses, famous phrases, the ingredients for french toast, and the names of people, places, and products. Your memorization of this information is useful.

How did you learn these handy words and numbers? Well, you first understood. You understood what dialing a certain phone number would do for you. You knew the taste of french toast and understood the convenience of making it without digging through a cookbook. You understood the value of your favorite automobile and you connected its name with your understanding of its value. Your understanding provided a motivation for memorization. And your memorization was not arduous dirty work. It came quite naturally.

And because your memorizations weren't accomplished through cramming, they stuck. And they continue to stick with you today because they have meaning and because you use them.

Can we approach knowing God's Word in a similar way? Indeed. Take a Scripture such as Romans 8:28: "We know that in everything God works for the good of those who love him." A thorough exploration of this passage produces understanding. We need to work carefully through the theology. Does the verse mean that God causes bad things to happen to us just so he can turn around and rescue us? Or does it mean that God takes the circumstances that naturally surround us and creates something good?

A skillful teacher will explore this verse, helping students work through their own life experiences. How has God taken their rough circumstances and produced resurrections? Students begin to interpret what happens around them in their everyday lives. They see God working. And Romans 8:28 takes on special meaning. They begin to experience the freedom of Christ—no matter what happens to them, God will be with them and bring them peace and ultimate good.

They recall Romans 8:28 because it has meaning in their lives, because they use it, and because they understand it.

Much of the rest of this book will supply you with strategies that produce understanding in your learners. Understanding of God's Word will help your people know, love, and follow Jesus.

> **"Over and over again, studies have demonstrated that we memorize best when we analyze what we are learning, find patterns in it, and relate it to knowledge we already have. In other words, when we think about it."**

—*David Perkins, Smart Schools* [7]

The "DO IT" section that follows offers practical programming ideas to help you share and apply these principles in your church.

To aid you in emphasizing understanding over rote memorization, here are teacher training tidbits to intersperse as reminders to focus on understanding.

Following the tidbits, you'll find ideas that help students find understanding in God's Word through unforgettable learning experiences.

TEACHER TRAINING TIDBITS

1. Recalling memory memories—Let teachers exchange stories from childhood when they had to memorize something at school or church. (This works best in pairs or trios.)

Help direct the discussion with thought-provoking questions:

● **Which subjects were easiest for you? most difficult? Why?**

● **Do you remember cramming for tests at any time in your life? Do you remember what you crammed? Did you understand the subject matter?**

● **Did you have a positive or negative experience memorizing Bible verses in childhood or teen years? What created that perception?**

● **When have you memorized something you didn't understand? Why does understanding play such a key role in learning?**

Use portions of this chapter to trigger further discussion. Have the original pairs or trios design three questions to ask the others in the group about the issue of rote memorization vs. understanding.

Plan and pray for ways to implement time for understanding God's Word in the classroom.

2. Exploring the issue—Photocopy the "What Does This Say?" handout on page 96. Let each person take a quick look at the page and read it. Ask what it says. Most people will read, "I love Paris in the springtime." (That's incorrect. There are two "the's.")

Point out that most people fail to see the second "the." They are so used to the phrase, "I love Paris in the springtime," that they can't imagine it any other way. It's called being "homeblind"—when people are too close to actually see things another way. Ask teachers to compare that experience with how people view memory work in the church. Are there flaws in your approaches to learning that are overlooked because you're homeblind?

Divide the "When Rote Runs Awry" section beginning on page 86 into four parts. Next create four groups and assign each group (a group can be one person) one of the "price tag" subsections: time, repellent, confusion, and hidden curriculum. Have the four groups each study their section and present their findings and discussion to the other three groups. Have them explore a new way to view biblical understanding in the classroom.

3. Roadblocks to understanding—The church is notorious for using a batch of foreign-sounding words that many don't understand. It's

WHAT DOES THIS SAY?

I

love

Paris in the

the springtime.

amusing, yet sad, when teachers and parents share stories of "cute" misunderstandings children make when it comes to the language. For instance, our 6-year-old son retold the story of Br'er Rabbit and repeated the part about the threat of being roasted on a stake. Matt thought the "stake" was a "steak," something to eat. And it didn't sound that bad to him! And when he was around two, he kept holding his hand to his nose whenever we talked about Noah's ark. We finally realized he understood "nose ark" not Noah's ark! It made sense to him! Another little girl buried her pet bird while praying, "In the name of the Father, Son, and in the hole he goes"!

Have teachers share similar stories of misunderstandings. Humorous as they may be, emphasize we're still after clarity and understanding when it comes to teaching in the church. To highlight the importance of understanding, try this:

Have teachers list words the church uses that people may not hear in their worlds outside of church; for example, Lord, righteousness, redemption, Trinity, Resurrection, trespasses, beseech. Divvy up the words among group members. Have people brainstorm ways to help children and adults understand those words. Or find ways to use words that are more recognizable.

ACTIVITIES TO MAKE SCRIPTURE STICK

Help teachers build their lessons around alternatives to rote memorization. Reinforce understanding of Scripture with activities such as these. They'll turn learning into an adventure. (The first two ideas, and 50 others, appear in the book *Making Scripture Stick* by Lisa Finn and Barbara Younger, Group Publishing. The last idea comes from *Snip-and-Tell Bible Stories* by Karyn Henley, Group Publishing.) The ideas are designed for school-age children but will add spice to youth or adult classes, too!

LEARNING ADVENTURE 1

BIBLE VERSE

"Then the King will answer, 'I tell you the truth, anything you did for even the least of my people here, you also did for me'" (Matthew 25:40).

PREPARING FOR THE ADVENTURE

Gather a length of clothesline, clothespins, slips of paper, and fine-point markers. Hang the clothesline at a height where kids can easily reach it. Contact a community shelter or agency that will accept charitable donations.

THE ADVENTURE

Have kids take off their shoes and pile them in the middle of the room, then sit in a circle around the shoes. Ask:

● **What would it be like to be without shoes?**

- **Where would it be difficult or embarrassing to go if you didn't have shoes?**
- **What else besides shoes do we need just to survive?**

Appoint two scribes and give them the slips of paper and markers. As kids name daily necessities of life, have the scribes write them on separate slips of paper. Other kids can clip the slips of paper onto the clothesline. Ask:

- **How do you think it would feel to go without one or two or three of these things?**

Read Matthew 25:40. Have kids repeat it with you. Ask:

- **Who is the King in this verse?**
- **Who are "the least of my people"?**
- **Why do you think Jesus said this?**
- **What do you think Jesus wants us to do?**

Say: **Jesus wants us to help those who have less than we do. Today we're going to start a project to collect something for needy kids. You're going to help decide what that something will be. Look at the suggestions on the clothesline. We'll vote on what you think we should collect.**

Have kids vote to choose what they'd like to collect. Explain where you'll be donating the collected items.

Then say: **Form pairs with one partner facing away from the shoe pile and the other partner facing the pile. The partner whose back is turned away from the pile will describe his or her shoes. The partner who's facing the pile will find and bring the shoes that fit the**

description. Then switch roles. Go!

When all the shoes have been retrieved, ask:

● **How is depending on your partner to bring you your shoes like the way needy people depend on us?**

Read Matthew 25:40 again.

REMEMBERING THE ADVENTURE

Have kids each take a clothespin from the clothesline and clip it to their shirt to remind them to bring their items for donations next week. You may want to put a note in the church bulletin or newsletter to share your project with the rest of the congregation.

LEARNING ADVENTURE 2

BIBLE VERSE

"God made peace through the blood of Christ's death on a cross" (Colossians 1:20).

PREPARING FOR THE ADVENTURE

Gather scrap lumber, nails, a hammer, 3×5 cards, markers, a tape of meditative worship music, and a cassette player. Make a wooden cross approximately 3 feet tall. Write the Bible verse on a 3×5 card and nail it to the center of the cross.

THE ADVENTURE

Lay the wooden cross on the floor and have kids sit in a circle around it. Ask:

● **What do you think of when you see a cross?**

● **Why did Jesus have to die?**

Distribute 3×5 cards and have each person write "Jesus died for the sins of (his or her own name)." As kids are writing, lay nails and a hammer beside the cross. Have kids take turns approaching the cross, reading the verse aloud, and nailing their cards to the cross. Play soft, meditative music and encourage kids not to talk, except when they read the verse.

When all the cards are nailed to the cross, ask:

● **How did you feel when you pounded your nail into the cross?**

Read Colossians 1:20. Close with sentence prayers. Go around the circle having kids say, "Thank you, Jesus, for dying for my sins."

REMEMBERING THE ADVENTURE

Distribute the leftover nails. Say: **Put your nail somewhere in your room. Each time you see it, remember that Jesus loves you so much that he was willing to die for you.**

LEARNING ADVENTURE 3

BIBLE VERSE

Jonah 1–2

PREPARING FOR THE ADVENTURE

You'll need scissors, one sheet of typing paper, and a marker.

THE ADVENTURE

With scissors and paper in hand, follow the diagrams shown on pages 103, 104, and 105. Then tell this story:

△ *(Fold the paper in half vertically.)*

One day God spoke to a man named Jonah. God said, "I want you to go to a city called Nineveh. Nineveh is a city full of people who do bad things. I want you to tell them to start doing what's right."

But Jonah didn't want to go. Was there ever a time when you didn't want to do what you were told to do? What did you do? *(Let children respond.)*

✂ Jonah decided to run away from God. He went to a city by the sea and got on a ship that was sailing far away. *(Cut figure from A to B.)*

But God knew what Jonah was doing. He sent a strong wind and a powerful storm. The waves beat against the ship. How do you think the sailors on that ship felt? *(Let children respond.)*

✂ The sailors were afraid the ship would break apart. They started throwing their boxes and baggage into the sea to make the ship lighter. *(Cut figure from B to C.)*

✂ The captain came to Jonah. "Why has this terrible storm come?" he asked. "Pray to your God. Maybe he'll help us!" *(Cut figure from C to D.)*

✂ Jonah said, "I know why this storm has come. It's because I'm running away from God." *(Cut figure from D to E.)*

✂ "What can we do?" asked the sailors. *(Cut figure from E to F.)*

✂ "You can throw me into the sea," said Jonah. *(Cut out section G. Unfold Jonah figure, hold vertically, and mark eyes on Jonah. Display Jonah and keep the whale figure horizontal so kids don't focus on it as you tell the next section of the story.)*

The sailors didn't want to throw Jonah into the sea. They tried to row the ship to the shore, but they couldn't. The storm only got worse. Finally they threw Jonah into the sea. Right away the storm stopped. The ship and the sailors were safe!

As for Jonah, God sent a huge fish to swallow him. *(Fold the Jonah figure down at his feet and fold the fish figure closed*

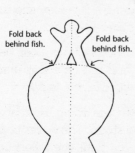

Fold back behind fish.

Fold back behind fish.

Hold the fish sideways to "swim" with Jonah inside.

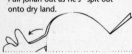
Pull Jonah out as he's "spit out" onto dry land.

again. Hold the figure horizontally to show the fish, with Jonah inside.)

While Jonah was inside the fish, he prayed, "I called to you, Lord. The waves came over me, but you saved me. I'll do what you asked me to do."

Then God told the fish to spit Jonah out and it did. Jonah was on dry land again! *(Still holding the fish horizontally, pull the Jonah figure out to show the fish spitting him out.)*

God said again, "Go to the city called Nineveh and tell the people what I told you to say before."

And this time, Jonah did!

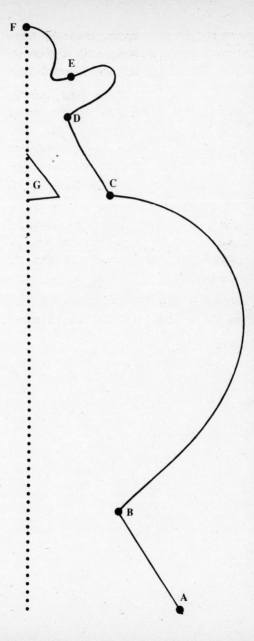

Diagram from *Snip-and-Tell Bible Stories*, copyright © 1993 Karen Henley. Reprinted by permission. Permission to photocopy this diagram granted for local church use. Copyright © Thom and Joani Schultz. Published in *Why Nobody Learns Much of Anything at Church: And How to Fix It* by Group Publishing, Inc., Box 481, Loveland, CO 80539.

5 MAKE PEOPLE THINK

Today's students have been trained not to think. They aren't dumber than previous generations. We've simply conditioned them not to use their heads.

You may have heard this old Sunday school story:

Teacher: All right, boys and girls, what's fuzzy, has a bushy tail, and gathers nuts in the fall?

Johnny: Sure sounds like a squirrel to me, but I know the answer must be Jesus.

You see, we've trained Johnny and his classmates to respond with the simplistic answers they think the teacher wants to hear. Fill-in-the-blank student workbooks and teachers who ask dead-end questions such as "What's the capital of Delaware?" have produced kids—and adults—who've learned not to think. We've programmed kids to look for snappy black-and-white answers that teachers want.

Researchers recently probed a group of second-graders in Birmingham, Alabama. These kids had just scored well above average on a statewide standardized math test. Now the researchers gave them this problem: *There are 26 sheep and 10 goats on a ship. How old is the captain?*

Ninety percent of the children gave the same answer: 36.[1]

We've withered kids' thinking and doused their common sense. What's more, we've chilled their creativity.

They're programmed to repeat what the workbook or teacher has prescribed. There's no room in this system to think "out of the box." Just say what the teacher wants to hear and forget about it.

Look at this typical problem from a child's reader:

The tightrope walker _____ on the tightrope.
a. balanced
b. baked
c. bubbled
d. barked

Students who check b, c, or d fail the question. But why should they fail? Think about those responses in b, c, and d. They conjure up far more creative thoughts than the response the teacher wanted. But no. The student is reprimanded for thinking, for being creative.

THE LAND OF THE R-BBIT

Our children are schooled very early not to think. Teachers attempt to help kids read with nonsensical fill-in-the-blank drills, word scrambles, and missing-letter puzzles. Educator Frank Smith calls these exercises "r-bbits." He coined the term (pronounced "are-bit") after attending the International Reading Association convention. A computer program was displayed that "helps kids read." The computer asked, "Can you fill in the missing letter in r-bbit?"

Smith says, "The r-bbit teaches children nothing about the way people employ spoken or written language. Filling in blanks is not the way anyone uses language, spoken or written. No one ever says to a child, 'Put on your _____, and we'll go to the game as soon as you guess the missing word.' The r-bbit is irrelevant and misleading."[2]

Sadly, the Christian world has followed secular education into this folly. Most Christian curricula consist of wall-to-wall r-bbits. Look at some actual examples from well-known denominational and independent Christian publishers:

Write these words in the correct spaces:
forgive   confess   sins

If we _____ our _____ to God, God will _____ us our sins. 1 John 1:9

Read the Bible verses and unscramble the words to answer the questions about trusting God:

Isaiah 40:28-29: What will God give those who are weak and tired?

W E R P O _____ and

G S T T H E R N _____

Remove the Ds, Ps, and Ks:

**K P C H R I S T I A N S D B E G A N P D T O K
M E E T K I N D T H E P C A T A C O M B S D P K
K P K D D P K K P D P K**

The writers of this material obscure God's Word; they intentionally hide the truth. This is what consumes our children's time in church. And we wonder why they don't understand even the most basic tenets of our faith?

Puzzles, scrambles, fill-in-the-blanks, and encoded messages do not promote thinking. They confuse and consternate. Through this type of meaningless busywork our students will not grow closer to God. They may, however, grow closer to winning a spot on *Wheel of Fortune*.

THE THINKING CHURCH

Some church leaders aren't altogether sure they want their people to think. They figure they've already done the thinking for their people. All their followers need to do is obey them. Without question.

But research shows that churches that encourage thinking produce more Christians with mature faith. However, those churches are in the minority. Only 46 percent of churchgoing adults say their church challenges their thinking. Only 42 percent of teenagers say their thinking is challenged in church.[3] And only 35 percent of fifth- and sixth-graders say their church classes make them think.[4]

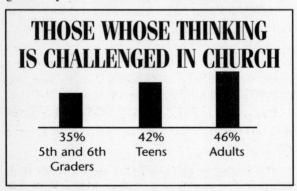

THOSE WHOSE THINKING IS CHALLENGED IN CHURCH

| 35% | 42% | 46% |
| 5th and 6th Graders | Teens | Adults |

Learning is a consequence of thinking. If our people aren't thinking, they're not growing in their faith. Christian educator Howard Hendricks says the average church attender "is not excited by the truth—he's embalmed by it. The educational program in the churches is often an insult to people's intelligence. We're giving them wilted cut flowers instead of teaching them how to grow by means of God's Word, which is alive!"[5]

PEOPLE WANT ANSWERS

"Today's people want answers. And here at First Church, we give them the answers."

Some churches advertise this almost boastful, arrogant attitude. The message seems to be "Ours is a black-and-white world. Come to our church with your questions, and we'll quickly dispense all the right answers and send you on your way."

Well, people today *are* seeking answers. But most aren't looking for quick and easy answers dispensed to them by authority figures. They want to *find* answers. They're weary of "just do it because I said so."

Search Institute's Christian education study found that young people said "teaching how to make moral decisions" is a chief responsibility of the church. Notice they did not ask for a list of the right decisions. They want us to teach them the skills to make their own good Christian decisions.

Our people don't need to be told *what* to think. But they desperately need to learn *how* to think in a Christian context.

Telling people what to think programs them to be susceptible to unhealthy influences around them. The church often warns teenagers of the dangers of peer pressure. But what is the result of peer pressure? It's the act of basing one's behavior on the influence of outside voices. It's the preclusion of thinking for oneself. The more we tell people what to think, the less they rely on their own thinking processes. The most authoritarian churches, the most authoritarian parents, produce the most peer-pressure-prone people.

We help our people grow not by giving them all the answers, but by helping them learn to think on their own. When they learn the process of finding God's direction in their lives, their learning becomes portable. They're able to learn and grow even when we teachers aren't around.

In Japan, where education has been shown to be more effective, students learn to think. As early as the first grade, Japanese students are given up to a week to solve arithmetic problems. They're encouraged to work together and critique each other's approaches. Teachers deliberately avoid supplying the answers. The kids learn. And they learn to think.

> **"Too much 'teacher talk' gets in the way of higher-level reasoning because it prevents children from doing their own thinking."**
>
> —*Jane Healy, Endangered Minds* [6]

JESUS THE ASKER

Jesus, the master teacher, displayed a determination to make his learners think for themselves. Even to this day followers contemplate and ponder Jesus' teachings. That's exactly how he planned it.

Jesus often refused to give a direct answer to a direct question. A lawyer once asked him, "Who is my neighbor?" Instead of supplying a direct answer, Jesus launched into a story about a Samaritan (Luke 10:29-37).

He used parables to make people think. And only rarely did he tell his listeners the meaning of his stories. He wanted them to think. And even today the mental wrestling we do helps us wring rich messages from Jesus' parables. And we grow more because we're engaged in the thinking process.

Many contemporary preachers also use parables. They call them sermon illustrations. But few preachers exhibit the faith in their listeners that Jesus did. Instead of telling their stories and sitting down, they usually go on to explain their stories. Their conviction of their flock's inability to think is a self-fulfilling prophecy. So long as Rev. Smith always explains his illustrations, no one needs to think. Might as well click off the old brain.

Jesus, on the other hand, believed in his listeners' ability to think, and he trusted the Holy Spirit to nudge their thinking. Jesus knew that once you plant a seed, you can trust God and the soil to do the rest.

"I planted the seed, and Apollos watered it. But God is the One who made it grow."

—The Apostle Paul in 1 Corinthians 3:6

Jesus also demonstrated his commitment to thinking by the number of questions he asked. We went through the gospels and highlighted every question Jesus asked. Those books are now a patchwork of yellow highlighter markings. Scores and scores of questions.

Often when people approached Jesus with a question he responded with a query of his own. One day in the temple, the priests and elders asked Jesus, "What authority do you have to do these things? Who gave you this authority?"

Jesus said, "I also will ask you a question. If you answer me, then I will tell you what authority I have to do these things. Tell me: When John baptized people, did that come from God or just from other people?" (Matthew 21:23-25). Those men were forced to think.

You see, Jesus didn't come to settle minds, but to jolt them. He didn't come to make us more comfortable, but to stir our thoughts, to help us learn, to make us think.

ASKING THE RIGHT QUESTIONS

So, we observe that Jesus was an asker. Step into any secular or church class and you'll find the teacher asking questions there too. What's the difference? There's a big difference.

Most teachers ask the wrong questions. We visited a typical first-grade Sunday school class and observed the teacher question her kids about Jesus' birth. She spent a significant portion of class time on this question: "Where was Jesus born?" Some of the kids eagerly thrust up their hands. "In heaven," said one. "In a hospital," said another. A little girl said, "On the earth."

The teacher said, "Yes, but where on the earth?"

"In Jerusalem?" inquired one child.

"No," said the teacher. "It was in Bethlehem. But where in Bethlehem?"

The questioning continued like this for several more minutes. The teacher had in mind a specific answer she wanted. The kids grew weary of her grilling and lost confidence in their ability to read the teacher's mind.

Finally, with a bit of desperation, the teacher tried to break the stalemate with a clue: "Jesus was born in a m-m-m-m-m-mmmmmm." The kids still didn't get it. The other teacher in the room finally jumped in and said, "He was born in a manger. As usual we're running out of time."

That's the kind of questioning that wastes time and chills thinking. Most of the class sits with dulled minds while one or two students try to reward the teacher with a factoid. That style of asking dominates the time in our churches and schools. One study found that fewer than 1 percent of teachers' questions elicit more than a factual answer or routine procedure.[7]

Asking students to recite facts from the Bible or elsewhere exercises just their memory, not their understanding. Even the scribes and the Pharisees knew the facts.

Instead of looking for a response such as "m-m-m-m-m-manger," why not try a thinking question? "Jesus was born in the cold where the animals were kept. What do you suppose that was like for him and his mother?" Each individual in the class can answer that question. Each is required to think, to contemplate the humble way in which Jesus came to earth.

Do you see the difference in goals between the two questions about Jesus' birth? The "m-m-m-m-m-manger" question sought a single student who might know that one-word answer, as in a TV game show. The "what do you suppose" question sought to make each child think, to imagine, to identify with Jesus.

Jesus didn't question his listeners in order to warehouse facts. He questioned them to make them think. Look at a few of his examples from the book of Matthew:

● *And why do you worry about clothes? (6:28)*

● *Why do you notice the little piece of dust in your friend's eye, but you don't notice the big piece of wood in your own eye? (7:3)*

● *Which is easier: to say, "Your sins are forgiven," or to tell him, "Stand up and walk"? (9:5)*

● *Why did you doubt? (14:31)*

● *What do you think about the Christ? (22:42)*

Christian educator and author Dorothy Jean Furnish says, "Avoid questions that require predetermined answers. This practice results eventually in hypocrisy on the part of children because they tell us what they think we want to hear."[8]

ENCOURAGING THINKING

Helping our people think requires a paradigm shift in how we teach. We need to plan for higher-order thinking, set aside time for it, and be willing to reduce our time spent on lower-order parroting, r-bbits, and the like.

Thinking classrooms look quite different from traditional classrooms. In most of our churches' nonthinking environments, the teacher does most of the talking in the hope that knowledge will somehow transmit from his or her brain to the students'. In thinking settings, the teacher coaches students to ponder, wonder, imagine, and problem-solve.

Let's examine five strategies you can implement right away that will encourage thinking in your church.

1. ASK OPEN-ENDED QUESTIONS.

"Where was Jesus born?" is a closed-ended question. This type of question is associated with lower-order thinking—memory, recall of facts. There's typically only one right answer to a closed-ended question. A student either knows the answer or not. And if he or she answers, the rest of the class will be uninvolved.

Open-ended questions require more than simplistic answers. They require students to think. And all students can be involved in the process. Thought-provoking, open-ended questions invite all to think, to listen to others' responses, and to contribute their own ideas. Open-ended questions cause people to use the content they've learned.

Some examples of open-ended questions:

● Why do you think God allowed Jesus, his only Son, to be born in a stable?

● If Jesus were born today, what kind of place would God choose for Jesus' birth?

● If, today, an unwed teenage girl gave birth to a boy in an alley, what would it take for you or anybody to believe he was the Messiah, the Son of God?

2. ASK FOLLOW-UP QUESTIONS.

Today's learners are conditioned to give pat answers—without thinking. But as teacher-coaches we don't have to settle for snap, no-brain responses. We can encourage thinking by asking follow-up questions. Some examples:

● What do you mean by...?
● What reasons do you have?
● How did you decide...?
● Tell me more.

Now, guess what you're likely to hear from time to time? "I don't know." This terribly common response is the battle cry of a generation that's been taught not to think. But, again, we don't have to settle for it. We can ask an extension question to "I don't know." Some samples from the book *Creating the Thoughtful Classroom:*

- Ask me a question that will help you understand.
- If you did know, what would you say?
- Pretend you do know—make something up.[9]

3. WAIT FOR STUDENTS' ANSWERS.

Today's teachers dread silence after they've asked a question. In fact, the average teacher waits only about one second before panicking. Then the teacher typically gives away an answer, rephrases the question, or scolds the students.

But thinking takes time. If we ask a good question we need to allow the time necessary for thinking to germinate. The minimum is five to 10 seconds.

We can make think time work by following some simple guidelines:

- *Tell your class or group what think time is, and why you use it.* It's no deep, dark teacher secret. You and your students will be more comfortable with silence if everyone knows its purpose.

- *Sometimes ask students to write their responses first. Then ask them to share.* This encourages everyone's participation—and soaks up the silence with active thinking.

- *Wait until most students have thought of a response before listening to anyone.* Always calling on Howie Hand-raiser shuts down thinking among the rest of the group. Use think time to allow everyone to devise a response.

4. DON'T EVALUATE STUDENTS' DISCUSSION RESPONSES.

This is the toughest guideline for us church folks. We

naturally want to affirm everyone. And we do that habitually in teaching situations. We love to say, "Good answer!" "Right!" and "Great!"

But think about it. What do those responses do to the rest of the class or group? They telegraph that the right answer has already been given—time to shut down the brain. Smarty Pants has already done the thinking and won the teacher's approval.

The authors of *Creating the Thoughtful Classroom* write, "Art Costa is a strong proponent of teaching without opinions, and he once demonstrated how the power of opinions can shut down thinking. He began a mock discussion and solicited ideas from his adult audience. Several responses later, he said 'good!' to an idea put forth. Within an instant, I could watch myself mentally shut down. I knew the person was 'right' and had given the answer he was looking for, and I didn't need to think any longer. Your students will do the same thing (and do already, all the time) if you selectively comment on students' responses."[10]

We must recognize that teacher reinforcement is powerful. We must use it wisely.

So how can we respond? We can use nonjudgmental responses such as "okay," "thank you," and "uh-huh." These responses acknowledge that students have been heard, without passing judgment, and without chilling thinking among the other students.

We can also reserve our opinions until the end of the discussion. After everyone has shared—and engaged their brains—we can help illuminate the subject with our thoughts or with an insight from God's Word. In this way students aren't encouraged to let the teacher do all the thinking.

But what if a student makes a theologically or morally

absurd statement? How do we handle that nonjudgmentally? At this point we can jump in with follow-up questions that may help the student and the class see the absurdity. We can also ask others to give their opinion. These techniques can help students discover the truth and flex their brains.

5. ENCOURAGE STUDENTS' QUESTIONS.

As we've seen, thinking percolates when teachers ask good questions. But a sure sign that thinking goes into four-wheel drive is when students begin to ask the questions.

And faith grows when people feel free to ask questions about God. Search Institute found that a church's "thinking climate" grows when members are encouraged to ask questions. However, most churches don't do too well in this department. Only 40 percent of adults and 45 percent of teenagers say their church encourages them to ask questions.[11]

When people become askers they become learners. They become thinkers.

We need to do a better job of inviting questions. And when those questions come we must resist the temptation to provide instant, pat answers. We must turn back the myth that our students will lose all respect for us if we sometimes answer their tough questions with "I don't know."

We must allow our people time to think, to wrestle with the issues. As Jesus often did.

And we can create a better thinking climate by encouraging students to ask one another questions. Let them forget we're the teachers for a while. Let them be the askers.

Educator and author Jane Healy says, "The teacher has to be able to stop dispensing information long enough to listen to the children, listen and encourage the children's questions."

THINKING IS ALIEN

Implementing these thinking strategies may not go smoothly at first. We're talking a new language here. Higher-order thinking is a new idea in the schools and in the church. Neither our kids nor our adults are accustomed to really thinking in church.

All of us grew up in the Land of Word Scrambles. We've all been trained to underuse our brains. But we've been vastly underestimated. Adults and children of all ages are capable of far deeper thinking than the system has expected of them.

So we must be patient. And we can't give up after our first attempt at cultivating thinking. Our people will at first stare at us like deer stunned in the headlights. But they'll come around. They'll grow to love the stimulation that thinking brings. And their faith will grow.

**"The mind is not a vessel to be filled,
but a lamp to be lit."**

—Anonymous

The "DO IT" section that follows offers practical programming ideas to help you share and apply these principles in your church.

DO IT Discover ways to create a thinking atmosphere in your church. The following ideas can spark teacher-training ideas, yet they can also be adapted to classrooms for older children, youth, and adults. In fact, taking students through some of these exercises will set the stage for greater thinking in the future—because students will understand why things are changing in the classroom. Go for it!

7 THINKING BOOSTERS

1. Develop a cadre of great askers. Teachers will need to shift from old ways of doing things. Delve into the "Encouraging Thinking" section beginning on page 116.

Plan to dissect each strategy by creating two different thinking approaches:

● **The "chills and kills" approach** uses closed-ended questions, doesn't wait for answers, and discourages further questions.

● **The "sparks and embarks" approach** uses open-ended questions and follow-up questions, allows wait time, and encourages questions.

Here's how to begin.

❏ Create five teams (a team can be one person). Assign each team one of the five portions of the "Encouraging Thinking" section:

(1) Ask open-ended questions.

(2) Ask follow-up questions.

(3) Wait for students' answers.

(4) Don't evaluate students' discussion responses.

(5) Encourage students' questions.

Have teams read and discuss their sections and prepare "classroom" scenarios that will teach the group their strategies.

❏ Assign each team a Scripture to portray in its classroom scenario. For example, use Genesis 11:1-9 (tower of Babel); Psalm 23 (shepherd's psalm); Matthew 4:1-11; (Jesus' temptation); Luke 15:1-7 (lost sheep); 1 Corinthians 13 (love chapter). Or assign only one passage to all the teams and see what each comes up with to represent its assigned strategy.

Have each team prepare two brief classroom scenarios to present to the entire group that demonstrate the point they studied. One scenario must represent the "chills and kills" thinking approach that shows *what not to do*—even though it may be typical or natural for most teachers. The second scenario must show the "sparks and embarks" thinking approach explained in their section of the chapter.

For example, the "chills and kills" scenario could show a teacher asking the students yes-or-no/fill-in-the-blank questions with only one excited, very interested student raising her hand to answer.

The "sparks and embarks" scenario could show a teacher asking open-ended questions that kids take time to think about then discuss with thoughtful responses.

❏ After each team "acts up," discuss the differences in the two scenarios. What's scary about the "chills and kills" scenario? Jot those fears on newsprint or a chalkboard for all to see. (Plan to use the list later in prayer.) Then create another written column of fears concerning the "sparks and embarks" scenario.

❑ Analyze the fear lists. Are there common threads? Who or what are people most afraid of? How can those fears be overcome? What's the Holy Spirit's role in the thinking process?

❑ Conclude with a circle prayer. Have each person pray about one of the fears on the lists.

2. Create a "safe" thinking place. Before you launch into requiring more student participation and thought, assess the class atmosphere. For example, is there one person who spouts theology and intimidates the less knowledgeable? Do the junior highers hurl put-downs that insult certain class members? Are there too many kindergartners for one teacher, so some feel trampled and left out? All these things could contribute to people not feeling "safe" to think.

Use the "Safe-Thinking Zone Ahead?" quiz on pages 125, 126, and 127.

3. Help students succeed by being very clear about your expectations. Together create a "covenant" or agreement for your class.

One successful teacher begins every year with one rule: RESPECT. Students explore respect and divide it into three categories: respect for the teacher, respect for one another, and respect for the facility. Together they decide what that means: what respect looks

SAFE-THINKING ZONE AHEAD?

Rate your learning setting by marking the appropriate box for each statement.

1. There's adequate adult supervision/leadership.
   ❏ Always ❏ Sometimes ❏ Never

2. People listen to the person speaking.
   ❏ Always ❏ Sometimes ❏ Never

3. People show respect in the way they talk to one another.
   ❏ Always ❏ Sometimes ❏ Never

4. People show respect in the way they act toward one another.
   ❏ Always ❏ Sometimes ❏ Never

5. The teacher shows respect to each person and each person's ideas.
   ❏ Always ❏ Sometimes ❏ Never

6. Expectations and rules are clear.
   ❏ Always ❏ Sometimes ❏ Never

7. Rules are few.
   ❏ Always ❏ Sometimes ❏ Never

8. People know the consequences if they violate the rules.
   ❏ Always ❏ Sometimes ❏ Never

9. The teacher models being a learner.
   ❏ Always ❏ Sometimes ❏ Never

10. Humor is used positively, never to put down a person or that person's thoughts.
    ❏ Always ❏ Sometimes ❏ Never

11. Everything that's taught and done has a clear purpose that aligns with your goal for learning in the church.
    ❏ Always ❏ Sometimes ❏ Never

12. Mistakes and failures are viewed as opportunities for growth and further learning.
    ❏ Always ❏ Sometimes ❏ Never

13. People feel a sense of trust in the group and are willing to take risks.
    ❏ Always ❏ Sometimes ❏ Never

14. People sense care and concern from others.
    ❏ Always ❏ Sometimes ❏ Never

Tally the number of boxes you checked for each:
    ___Always ___Sometimes ___Never

● If most of your boxes said "Never," you've got a long road ahead to change the atmosphere to a safe one. Find a support person or group of people who'll help you make the significant changes necessary. Train students to strive for the 14 items listed in the quiz. With God's help and the help of others it is possible to change and bring people on board for a new, more exciting, life-changing approach to learning.

● If most of your boxes said "Sometimes," congratulations! You've got a good start. People in learning situations understand the tip of the "safe" iceberg. Continue to verbalize the 14 items listed in the quiz. This will help train others to focus on the same goal, so you can move more toward "Always."

● If most of your boxes said "Always," GREAT! You've obviously worked hard to achieve trust and clear boundaries. Keep it up and use the 14 items listed on the quiz to help others join in your "safety" cause. You've mastered a safe zone for thinking!

like, sounds like, and feels like in each category. Next they design a colorful poster with the word "respect" on it, plus their definitions. Once it's completed, each person signs the poster as a commitment to respect. Since the teacher has used this activity, the classes have run more smoothly and the atmosphere is more conducive to thinking.

Here's a list of expectations that promote thinking among students. Talk about the list. Don't keep it a secret! Let people know how important these elements are to the success of the class. You'll commit to doing the best you can and expect the same in return. Help students develop these skills:

● listen to one another
● participate
● take time to think—and feel okay about that
● give reasons for answers
● stay on the task or topic
● ask thought-provoking questions

4. Study how Jesus asked questions. Turn teachers into detectives. Do a Bible study that explores Jesus' question-asking techniques. Have teachers pair up and divide one gospel (Matthew, Mark, Luke, or John) into sections among the group. Or if you have four groups, assign one gospel to each group. Have groups list on paper every question Jesus asked in their portion of Scripture. Encourage teachers to analyze why the question was so effective or powerful in each setting. What can they learn about formulating questions after studying Jesus' questions?

5. Learn to phrase thought-provoking questions. In the book *Endangered Minds* by Jane Healy, the author speaks of children lacking experience with "wh" questions (who, what, when, where, why, and how). "Studies demonstrate that educating teachers in specific questioning techniques can improve their students' reading comprehension, among many other skills, by moving their thinking up from literal repetition of facts into the realms of comprehension, application, and inferential reasoning."[12] Here are samples of some particular types of questions:

Closed-ended question: "What did Goldilocks do when she got to the three bears' house?"

Comprehension question: "Why did Goldilocks like the little bear's chair best?"

Application question: "If Goldilocks had come into your house, what are some of the things she might have used?"

Analysis question: "How can we tell which things belong to which bear?"

Synthesis question: "How might the story be different if Goldilocks had visited the three astronauts?"

Evaluation question: "Do you think Goldilocks had a right to do what she did? Why or why not?"[13]

Share the preceding information with teachers. Discuss each kind of question. Have teachers each bring their curriculum teachers guide to review. Where there are closed-ended questions, replace them with comprehension, application, analysis, synthesis, or evaluation questions.

For fun, star all the questions in the teachers guides that require higher-order thinking. Count them and see how the questions rate on making people think. How much of it do you have to adapt?

For additional flexing, assign teachers various Scripture passages and have them devise thought-provoking questions for them.

6. Develop a list of tips for thought-full teachers and classrooms. Together, brainstorm ideas that will help students and teachers create a thinking atmosphere. Discussion-time ideas could include:

● *Write questions on the board or newsprint for all to see.* (Since most people are visual learners, this helps learners focus on questions that might otherwise be lost because they're handled only orally.)

● *Explain to students upfront what you're up to.* (Let students know you're trying something new and why. Let them join in making a thinking classroom happen.)

● *Tell students you'll wait for answers.* (Good questions mean people will need time to formulate answers.)

● *Let students know you'll be giving them feedback on their answers with words such as "thank you" and "uh-huh."* (If they're used to you gushing praise on their answers, this will help them understand you aren't disappointed with them; you just want to make sure everyone gets a chance to think before assuming the "right" answer has already been given.)

● *Explain the use of small group interaction.* (Chapter 7 will address that in depth.)

7. Challenge teachers to break old habits.
If teachers want to improve their ability to ask better questions, they can:

● Use an audio or video cassette to record their classes. This will help "play back" the reality of what's asked during class time. (Those who've done this warn teachers not to be too hard on themselves. Don't pick at each little infraction; rather, evaluate the scope of what's asked and ways to improve.)

● Invite someone they respect to be their "observer." This person can watch and analyze classroom interactions that the teacher might overlook. They can spend time processing the class with their observers, celebrating their successes, and growing from their weaknesses.

● Invite students to listen for closed-ended questions and point them out to the teacher during class. (One courageous teacher who tried this technique gave points to students who recognized closed-ended questions. She discovered this not only helped her, but got students to really listen!)

● Find a support system. Get together with other teachers who are trying new teaching methods. It'd make a great support group at church.

Then work on improving bit by bit. Don't give up. Remember, we've gone for years and years teaching a certain way. It's not easy to break old patterns. And it takes time to develop new habits.

Let God's words, "Well done, good and faithful servant!" ring in your heart.

6 USE ACTIVE LEARNING

A ctive learning is, quite simply, learning by *doing*. It differs greatly from the methodology typically overused in the church—passive learning.

Sunday school kids sit around a long table. The teacher lectures. The kids stare at yet another Bible crossword puzzle in their student books. It's the same routine week in and week out. Few learn and fewer look forward to coming. The scene looks the same in our secular schools.

Lynn Stoddard studied how the human brain works for his book *Redesigning Education*. He says:

"The workbooks, worksheets, and textbooks that are an integral part of the drill-test syndrome cause anxieties or boredom, which in turn causes human brains to shut down or to learn that schooling is irrelevant to life."[1]

It's different in Japanese schools, where students learn more. The classrooms are lively, loud, and active. They do not fit the stereotype most Americans hold of Asian schools. Japanese lessons are not rote. Teachers spend little time lecturing. Students are not passive receptacles but active participants in the learning process.

Japanese classes are hands-on. Students learn by doing. Newsweek magazine describes a typical Tokyo elementary classroom: "The room is bedlam. Kids squirm, punch, scribble as they work in pairs, guessing the weight of pencils, mirrors, compasses, and then moving teeny weights on and off a balance. No one cracks a textbook. No child is a mere observer. No child takes notes. The lesson goes from fingertips to brain."[2]

Does that sound like the kind of classroom you remember in grade school? Western schools chose the passive model. And the church puppy-dogged along behind, never questioning if there might be a better way.

"The model of learning as transmission of information from teacher to student is bankrupt," says Brian Drayton at the Technical Education Research Center in Cambridge, Massachusetts. His nonprofit organization is developing new math and science curricula that use active-learning principles.

WHAT IS ACTIVE LEARNING?

Aircraft pilots know well the difference between passive and active learning. Their passive learning comes through listening to flight instructors and reading flight instruction books. Their active learning comes through actually flying the airplane or flight simulator. Books and lectures may be helpful, but pilots will tell you they really learned to fly by manipulating the plane's controls themselves.

We can look at learning in the church in a similar way. Though we may engage our students passively in some reading and listening to teachers, their understanding and application of God's Word will really take off through actual and simulated experiences.

An example: The youth worker grows concerned over

the formation of cliques within his youth group. He sees kids excluding their peers, particularly newcomers. He delivers a sermon about how God wants us to be accepting of others—cliques are destructive.

That's a passive learning approach to the problem. Now let's consider an active-learning approach.

The youth worker divides the group into subgroups of six. He asks each subgroup to form a circle. One of the six is asked to step outside the circle while the remaining five lock arms. The kids are told to keep the "outsiders" from entering their circles. What ensues is a raucous blur of pulling, squeezing, tickling, and laughing. Some of the outsiders battle their way into their circles. Others try but fail. One gives up and sits in the corner.

Now the youth worker beckons the kids to sit and process what they just experienced. He asks the outsiders, "How did you feel being locked out of your group?" And he asks the clique groups, "How did you feel locking out your outsider?" Then he probes a little deeper: "How is that little experience like what happens at school or right here in our youth group?"

The kids begin to open up. Light bulbs click on in their heads. They begin to understand the destructiveness of their past behavior. They learn. And their behavior changes.

That's active learning.

Other forms of active learning include simulation games, role-plays, service projects, experiments, research projects, group pantomimes, mock trials, purposeful games, and field trips.

This style of learning can be used week in and week out in the church.

WHY USE ACTIVE LEARNING?

In our interviews with grade school children, we learned that what they like least about Sunday school is "sitting in chairs." They've grown very weary of teacher talk and pointless seat work in student workbooks. And they know they're not learning.

And the problem is not limited to young children. Abundant research has shown that people of any age learn relatively little through passive-learning methods. The very methods the church has chosen to emphasize—lecture and reading—are those that bear the least fruit.

Edgar Dale, former professor of education at Ohio State University, conducted a classic study of the effectiveness of various teaching tools. He ranked these 10 methods in the form of a cone, with the most effective appearing at the base. (See the diagram on page 137.)

"The Cone of Experience" depicts a variety of learning approaches, all of which can prove successful in the church. Each can be enhanced by supplementing the teaching with other methods on the scale.

The top of the cone shows learning methods that rely on other people's experiences. These methods require little student involvement and result in relatively little learning.

The bottom shows methods that require the learner to experience certain situations. "Direct, purposeful, personal experiences" depend on the full involvement of the learner—senses, mind, and body. This type of experience would include a church class that decides to study servanthood by preparing and delivering a special meal to a shut-in. This level of involvement results in maximum learning.

"Contrived experiences" provide almost as much learn-

THE CONE OF EXPERIENCE

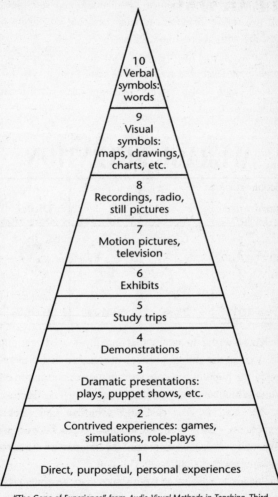

10 Verbal symbols: words

9 Visual symbols: maps, drawings, charts, etc.

8 Recordings, radio, still pictures

7 Motion pictures, television

6 Exhibits

5 Study trips

4 Demonstrations

3 Dramatic presentations: plays, puppet shows, etc.

2 Contrived experiences: games, simulations, role-plays

1 Direct, purposeful, personal experiences

ing potential as direct, purposeful, personal experiences. These contrived activities can be performed in the classroom at any time. Games, simulations, and role-plays, when carefully planned and later debriefed, can result in learning with lasting implications.

Studies reveal that the more students become involved in an experience, the more they'll learn from it. The following chart shows average retention rates of different learning methods.[3]

AVERAGE RETENTION

Spoken or written communication	Media	Role-Play	Direct experience
5-10%	25%	40-60%	80-90%

It's sobering to admit that our most used learning methods in the church produce the least results. Relentlessly we hope our people will memorize and retain all we tell them and assign them to read.

We—the church—have underachieved. Our people don't know what they should, and their lives are not deeply affected because we've clung to the old, passive ways by which we were taught.

Imagine if we'd try to teach someone to use a computer with the methodology we use in the church. Listen to a lecture on computers, try to unscramble the word "megabyte," look at the manual, memorize it—then go turn on the

LEARNING STYLES

Each of us favors certain stimuli to help us learn. Some of us depend more on our ears. Some of us rely more on our eyes, and so on. We're all different. We possess different learning styles. In any classroom, youth group, or congregation, you'll find a kaleidoscope of individuals with different learning styles. In order to help everyone learn, we must vary our learning approaches. Good active-learning curricula cover all learning styles.

Here's a brief description of the three basic learning styles:

1. Visual—These learners depend mainly on their eyes. They tend to remember what they see. They may remember a face but not a name.

2. Auditory—These learners rely on their ears to receive and process information. They may remember a name but not a face.

3. Kinesthetic—These learners prefer movement. They remember what they do, touch, and feel.

machine. Nobody learns to use a computer that way!

Learning the computer requires jumping in and trying some stuff. Manipulating the controls. Experiencing the joy of making it work. Suffering through the frustrations of little failures. Discovering new capabilities and useful applications.

The best way to learn the computer—and most anything—is through active learning.

Please don't misunderstand. Learning methods such as

listening to lectures and sermons have their place. And reading the Word is essential. But we've tended to place all our hopes in these passive methods. And we've almost completely ignored the more potent forms of learning.

People of any age learn best by doing—working hands-on with resources and other people, building on what they already know.

"Tell me and I'll forget. Show me and I may remember. Involve me and I'll understand."
—*Anonymous*

CHARACTERISTICS OF ACTIVE LEARNING

We can more fully explain active learning by exploring four characteristics.

1. ACTIVE LEARNING IS AN ADVENTURE.

What turns an ordinary family vacation into an adventure? It's when the unexpected happens! When embarking on an active-learning experience, the outcome can't be completely predicted. You never know exactly what will happen. It's an adventure!

We've done the clique experience mentioned earlier dozens of times—with kids and adults. But we can never predict what will happen. At one church council retreat the pastor climbed atop a table and dived headfirst into the clique circle. Nothing would stop him from being in the middle of things! A very revealing discussion followed. We couldn't have predicted that outcome. But real learning took place.

Passive learning, however, is almost always predictable: Students sit passively while the teacher or speaker follows a planned outline or script.

> **"It's so painful to go into many of**
> **our churches and Sunday school**
> **classes and Bible study groups—**
> **they're so predictable you can**
> **fall asleep, wake up 10 minutes later,**
> **and find them exactly where you**
> **expected them to be."**
>
> —*Howard Hendricks* [4]

In active learning, people may learn lessons the teacher never envisioned. Because the teacher trusts students to help create the learning experience, learners may venture into unforeseen discoveries. And often the teacher learns as much as the students.

2. ACTIVE LEARNING IS FUN AND/OR CAPTIVATING.

Today's adults often grumble about the younger generation. "I get so frustrated with these kids," they say. "They're great at playing games and having fun. But when it's time to get serious and learn, they want no part of it."

One Christian education director told us, "I tell my kids if they don't want to get into hard-core, serious Bible study, they can just leave."

And they do.

What are we communicating when we say, "Okay, the fun's over—time to talk about God"? What's the hidden curriculum? The message kids take with them: Joy is separate from God. And learning is separate from joy.

What a shame.

Many people assume that fun and learning cannot occur at the same time. Once again, they learned this from their own educational upbringing. As kindergartners they found school to be colorful, fun, and captivating. But by third or fourth grade they got the message: Fun and learning don't mix. Along the way, well-meaning teachers confused students' boredom for lack of ability. But sadly, it was the teachers' own lack of ability that squeezed the fun out of learning.

> **"If there's a general malaise in American education today, it has more to do with student boredom than intellectual capacity."**
>
> —*John Naisbitt* [5]

We often hear, "You shouldn't have to entertain kids to get them to learn." That comment reveals someone who's forgotten the goal. You see, the methodology (that is, entertaining vs. nonentertaining) is not the goal. It's simply a means to the goal. If your goal is to help people grow closer to God, you'll be open to methodologies that achieve that goal—including methodologies that work because they're entertaining.

In American education, fun has acquired a bad name. But not in a remarkable school in northern Italy. The Reggio Emilia school uses the slogan, "Niente Senza Gioia." Translated, it's "Nothing Without Joy." The faculty assures that a joyful, playful, creative spirit permeates the school, right from the first day. And this school has created a world-class learning environment.

Active learning is fun and/or captivating. A fifth-grader we interviewed clearly remembered her "best" Sunday school lesson. Crystal described it, "Jesus was the light and we went into a dark room and we shut off the lights. We had a candle and we learned that Jesus is the light and the dark can't shut off the light." That's active learning. Crystal enjoyed the lesson. She had fun. And she learned.

Active learning intrigues people. When they find a foot-washing experience captivating or maybe a bit uncomfortable, they learn. And they learn on a deeper level than any r-bbit worksheet or teacher's lecture could ever reach.

3. ACTIVE LEARNING INVOLVES EVERYONE.

There are no passive spectators in active learning. Here the difference between passive and active learning becomes abundantly clear. It's like the difference between watching a football game on television and actually playing in the game.

Yes, you'll learn a little bit about a football game by watching it on television. But you'll learn far more and remember the game longer if you put on the pads and helmet and run onto the field and play.

The "trust walk" provides a good example of involving everyone in active learning. Half the group dons blindfolds; the other half serves as guides. The "blind" people trust the guides to lead them through the building or outdoors. The guides prevent the blind people from falling down stairs or tripping over rocks. Everyone needs to participate to learn the inherent lessons of trust, faith, doubt, fear, confidence, and servanthood. Passive spectators of this experience would learn little. Participants learn much.

4. ACTIVE LEARNING IS FOCUSED THROUGH DEBRIEFING.

Activity simply for activity's sake doesn't usually result in good learning. That's why we need to follow our activities with meaningful discussion—debriefing.

Without debriefing, the trust walk described above may linger in students' memories as merely an interesting exercise. To draw real Christian understanding from this experience, debriefing as a group is necessary.

Debriefing—or evaluating an experience by discussing it in pairs or small groups—helps focus the experience and draw out its meaning. Debriefing helps sort and order the information students gather during the experience. It helps learners relate the just-experienced activity to their lives.

The process of debriefing is best started immediately

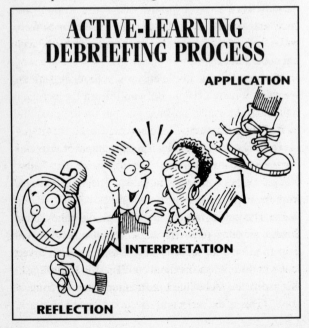

ACTIVE-LEARNING DEBRIEFING PROCESS

APPLICATION

INTERPRETATION

REFLECTION

after an experience. This also holds true for those teachable moments—unexpected times when your students are ready to learn. Simply gather your learners and say, "Hey, let's talk about what just happened here."

We use a three-step process in debriefing: reflection, interpretation, and application.

A. Reflection—This first step asks the students: *"How did you feel?"* Active-learning experiences typically evoke emotions. So, it's appropriate we begin our debriefing there.

Some people ask, "What do feelings have to do with education?" Feelings have everything to do with education. Think back to a time in your life when you really learned a big lesson. In all likelihood strong feelings accompanied that time. Our emotions tend to cement things into our memory.

When you're debriefing, use open-ended questions to probe feelings. Avoid questions that can be answered with a yes or no. Let your learners know that there are no wrong answers to these reflection questions. Everyone's feelings are valid.

B. Interpretation—The next step in the debriefing process asks: *"What does this mean to you? How is this experience like some other aspect of your life?"* Now you're asking people to identify a message or principle from the experience.

Let's say you teach a class of first-graders. One Sunday morning you break out an ice cream bar and eat it in front of your students. You observe their starved looks as you polish off the ice cream. First you'll ask, "How did you feel while I ate that ice cream in front of you?" (This is the reflection question.) Then you'll ask,

"How is what just happened here like when you don't share your things with other children?" That's the interpretation question—connecting the fresh experience with some other aspect of life.

Now you want your learners to discover the message. Rather than telling students your answers, take the time to ask questions and encourage self-discovery. Use Scripture and discussion in pairs or small groups to explore how the actions and effects of their activity might translate to their lives.

Alert! Some of your people may interpret wonderful messages you never intended. That's not failure! That's the Holy Spirit at work. God allows us to catch different glimpses of his kingdom, even though we all may be looking through the same glass.

C. Application—The final debriefing step asks: *"What will you do about it?"* This step moves learning into action.

Your people have shared a common experience. They've discovered a principle. Now they must create something new with what they've just experienced and interpreted. They must integrate the message into their lives.

The application stage of debriefing calls for commitment. Ask your students how they'll change, how they'll grow, and what they'll do as a result of your time together.

Too often we neglect commitment in the church. We may be diligent about selling our people on something, but we're timid about "closing the sale." We may robustly preach, "Love your neighbor," but we rarely ask individuals to pledge how they'll live out that Christian message next week.

Really, none of us accomplishes anything without

commitment. If we want Christian growth in our people, we must ask for their commitment.

The debriefing process creates a superb environment for commitment. We have witnesses! Commitments made without the scrutiny of witnesses typically get broken and forgotten. Witnesses provide accountability.

Within debriefing pairs or small groups we can ask for commitment in many ways. We can call for oral commitment. Each person can publicly answer a simple question, such as "How will today's experience on cliques affect how you'll act in our group from now on?"or "Who's one person you'll call this week and invite to our group?"

Commitment can also come during prayer time, with each person asking aloud for God's help in accomplishing some goal.

And commitments can be written. The written commitments can be kept in a certain place, or exchanged with partners, or collected by the teacher and mailed to the students a month later as a motivating reminder.

> **"Knowledge is experience. Everything else is just information."**
> —*Albert Einstein*

ACTIVE LEARNING AND THE LEARNING DISABLED

Educators estimate that up to 20 percent of today's students possess some type of learning disability such as attention deficit disorder (ADD). The church has done no favors for students with learning disabilities. R-bbits, word scrambles, and puzzles are not entertaining learning devices for kids with learning disabilities. They're tortuous gobbledygook.

Passive, lecture-based classrooms leave the learning disabled several steps behind. Their minds are still trying to untangle the teacher's first words while the class speeds ahead on a "more is better" cram ride.

Kids with learning disabilities often suffer from more than their share of low self-esteem. Passive, teacher-based classrooms and endless r-bbits seem to magnify their disabilities. Their frustration grows to sometimes explosive levels. And they convince themselves they're stupid and worthless.

Students with reading disabilities such as dyslexia perceive letters and words as jumbled. The letter "d" may look like a "b". To help you understand what those with reading disabilities endure, we've simulated a sentence to appear as it might to a person with a learning disability:

Apaw ang Evel iveb inGob's garb encallep egen.

What does it say? Imagine a teacher insisting that you read that sentence aloud in a Sunday school class. How would you feel?

The jumbled sentence above actually represents this sentence: Adam and Eve lived in God's garden called Eden.

The written word is hard enough for kids with reading disabilities. But the use of word jumbles, fill-in-the-blanks, puzzles, and word searches are downright cruel to these students. And totally unnecessary.

Traditional Sunday school work sheets require sequential thought processes. The first concept or task in a sequence must be thoroughly grasped before the following thoughts or concepts make sense. Thinking sequentially is extremely difficult for students with learning disabilities such as ADD. In fact, half of *all* students are frustrated by sequential assignments. They're more global and random in their organization and processing of information. And that provides another good reason to use active learning in Christian eduaction.

Active learning opens new and freeing windows for the learning disabled. Good active learning involves all the senses. And kids with learning disabilities who may be poor auditory learners can still pick up active learning's Bible lessons through other more preferred senses.

And because kids with learning disabilities are more successful and more captivated in the active-learning classroom, they're less of a discipline problem. Traditional church teachers often become extremely frustrated with some "hyper" kids who always seem to be out of control. Many of these so-called problem kids are actually children with learning disabilities whose needs are not being met by the ineffective teaching methodologies used in the class. But when teachers switch to active learning, these same kids become far more manageable because they're engaged and they're moving at their own pace.

What a special ministry the church can provide to kids with learning disabilities! And it can be accomplished without treating them differently or separating them from their friends.

Active learning works—for all types of learners.

JESUS THE ACTIVE TEACHER

Jesus was a master teacher. He used a variety of learning approaches. As a young boy he modeled the value of reading God's Word. And as an adult he used his powerful gift of oratory. He never wrote a book. He trusted that the potency of his encounters with people would be remembered and transmitted through the ages.

Jesus immersed people in experiences of all kinds—healing some, feeding others, and casting out demons in still others. He manipulated the weather to teach his disciples a lesson (Matthew 8:23-27).

He loved to teach with the interesting materials around him. He didn't use fill-in-the-blank work sheets. He used dirt, water, wine, clothing, trees, grains of wheat, sheep, goats, boats, nets, fish, little children, and a Roman coin—the paraphernalia of his day.

And Jesus knew people learned by doing. To teach his disciples a lesson on servanthood, he dropped to his knees and began washing their feet. He could have preached an eloquent sermon on servanthood. But he knew the power of experience. He knew his men would best understand if they *experienced* this lesson.

And his disciples, much like the church today, objected to Jesus' active learning methodology. Peter blurted, "No! You will never wash my feet!" He would have been much more comfortable passively listening to a sermon.

But Jesus persisted. In fact, he said, "You don't understand now what I am doing, but you will understand later" (John 13:7). Read that quote again. It's the essence of active learning. Big lessons come through life experiences. And often we don't even realize we're learning something profound. Reflecting on an experience focuses and cements its lesson in our hearts. After the foot washing, Jesus asked, "Do you understand what I have done for you?"

Jesus understood the workings of the human mind. He knew the disciples would never grasp servanthood or

God's nature until they experienced something dramatic. He could have explained the concept, but he wanted to deliver a knockout punch they'd never forget.

Yes, Jesus used storytelling and other more passive forms of teaching. But he creatively interspersed these with lots of active-learning episodes, thereby strengthening and galvanizing a message that will live forever.

THE FEARS OF ACTIVE LEARNING

Active learning is not a passing fad. It's a proven, effective methodology. Jesus used it to perfection. But many church folk are scared of it. Why? Let's look at some common fears.

FEAR #1: TOO RISKY

Some teachers and preachers say letting people discover learnings from active experiences is too risky. "At least I know that when I give a talk, people are getting some real meat." Don't be so sure. Lecturing is extremely risky. Many people aren't concentrating on the speaker. Those who are listening will forget most of the speaker's words before they have a chance to apply them.

Others place their confidence in student workbooks and fill-in-the-blanks. "The information is all there. It's complete and exact," they say. But factoids on a page do not magically change students' behavior. Most people quickly forget almost everything they read on student work sheets. Relying on r-bbits is very risky business indeed.

But teachers still fret about active learning. "What if they don't get the point I'm trying to get across?" Well, maybe they'll learn something *better* than what the teacher intended. Active learning allows students to learn different truths from the same experience. Can we not trust the Holy Spirit to guide our learners?

The Bible is filled with active-learning experiences, each requiring trust that the learners would "catch it": Abraham and Isaac, Jonah, the Flood, the wedding at Cana, the storm on the lake, the woman caught in adultery, the question of taxes, healing on the Sabbath. Pretty risky lessons.

If God can risk with active learning, maybe we can, too.

FEAR #2: TEACHER WISDOM WASTED

Some folks view active learning as "the blind leading the blind." Without the teacher's lecture, without the student workbook, they fear the students will simply pool their ignorance.

In active learning, teachers don't check out. They *do* offer their wisdom and insight. But not in a formal lecture or sermon. During the debriefing time, teachers share right along with students. As members of the group they have a right to be heard. And in this informal setting, in small groups, teachers' insights carry more weight. They're speaking personally from the heart, not putting on a show from behind a podium.

FEAR #3: TOO NOISY

When first observing an active-learning session, some teachers may cringe. "You call this learning? There's noise and chaos and laughter!" they say.

Well, yes, we must admit active learning will occasionally result in a higher noise level. But whoever decreed that learning best takes place in a quiet, passive room?

Child magazine recently published its selection of the 10 best schools in America. One of them was Public School 87 in New York City. The description: "Walk down the halls and you won't even hear your heels click on the linoleum. Instead, children's voices fill the air. Teachers' voices can also be heard above the din, making this a very noisy school indeed. In no classroom were children seated at desks while teachers barked instructions."[6]

Bev Bos, a nationally renowned California preschool teacher, was featured on ABC's *20/20* news show. She said, "I'm appalled when I see kids sitting on their bottoms and the teachers going on and on and on and everybody's going, 'Sh, sh, sh, sh, sh, sh, sh.' "[7]

Mark, a fifth-grade Sunday school teacher, recently began using Group Publishing's Hands-On Bible Curriculum™. Before he switched to this active-learning curriculum he said he "spent half the time getting the kids to quiet down. Now I don't have to discipline them much anymore. They still make noise. But their noise is learning noise. They really get involved in the lesson."

FEAR #4: LOSS OF CONTROL

This one is akin to the noise fear. Some teachers worry that if students get out of their chairs, a riot may break out. Teachers feel more comfortable standing in command before silent, still, passive receptacles of teacher knowledge.

But watching students sit still in chairs is not our goal. Control is not the goal. Learning is the goal. And learning readily happens amidst activity.

The whole issue of control in youth and children's classrooms has been overemphasized and misunderstood in the church. Kids want to move about and expend energy for a simple reason—that's the way they're made! They're kids! That's what kids do. They're 50,000-watt bundles of exuberance. That pep has to come out somehow. And we adults spend our time trying to devise schemes to hermetically seal kids' energies. It's a hopeless effort.

Active learning gives kids (and adults) positive, appropriate outlets for their natural energy. Since they have opportunities to burn some energy, they're more likely to focus their thoughts when it's time for debriefing. And this is why active-learning teachers actually complain less about discipline problems than passive teachers.

FEAR #5: FAILURE

Some teachers fear that an active-learning experience may not turn out as expected. "What if this thing flops?"

The beauty of active learning is that quality education can occur no matter how the activity goes. Skillful active-learning teachers can produce times of great learning out of even the most miserable apparent failures.

One teacher tried a foot-washing experience with his teenagers. He expected meaningful learning to occur when the kids removed their shoes and received his act of servanthood. But "failure" swept over the experience when one belligerent guy, Rick, refused to remove his shoes. In the midst of this awkward moment the leader almost wished he'd given his old talk on servanthood instead of risking this failure-prone, active-learning stuff.

But this leader sensed a teachable moment. He asked the group, "How do you feel right now?" After a brief silence, one of the kids asked Rick why he wouldn't remove his shoes. Rick swallowed hard and said, "Um, I'm really embarrassed. My feet are really ugly. I don't want anybody to see them."

What followed allowed Rick to experience God's unconditional love. Up until then Rick had felt like a misfit in the group. One by one the kids expressed their acceptance and love for Rick. "It doesn't matter what your feet look like. We love you just as you are," said one of the kids.

After that "failed" bit of active learning, Rick was never the same. Instead of being a fringe group member, he got involved. Today Rick is a minister.

> ## "I don't believe we learn by our triumphs. I think we learn by our mistakes."
>
> —*Chuck Jones, creator of Wile E. Coyote* [8]

FEAR #6: PEOPLE WILL GET TIRED OF IT

Passive-learning teachers often express this fear. They don't understand.

After employing active learning for more than 20 years we've never heard even one learner say, "Gee, I sure get tired of doing something new every week. Couldn't we go back to the old lectures and student workbooks?"

Passive learning—not active learning—is what tires out learners. Kids and adults are tired—sick and tired— of lectures, word scrambles, and r-bbits.

Active learning, by its very nature, offers variety and unpredictability. Each active experience can be different, utilizing different senses, different emotions, different discoveries. And, active-learning sessions include a variety of activity levels. The active experiences can be interspersed with quieter times, debriefing, discussion, Bible work, and prayer. The chances for boredom and predictability are slim indeed.

You can learn much more about active learning in our book *Do It! Active Learning in Youth Ministry.*

The "DO IT" section that follows offers practical programming ideas to help you share and apply these principles in your church.

What really works in active learning? The next few pages offer a smorgasbord of ideas for all ages. Even though all the experiences contain the ingredients of active learning, we've arranged them to highlight specific aspects of the active-learning process. Try them out. And celebrate the joy of discovery!

ADVENTURE IDEAS

"Adventure" holds the aura of excitement, the unknown, and a pioneering spirit. Here are four activities that do just that.

● **Bethlehem revisited**—Turn the Christmas season into a wonderful learning adventure. Research what it must have been like 2,000 years ago in Bethlehem—the streets, the food, the clothing. With all ages involved as shepherds, vendors, potters, and the like, re-enact what it was like when Jesus was born. Turn the church classrooms or parking lot into shops, eateries, a too-full inn, a stable, and a field. Let visitors wander from place to place to discover Bethlehem. Make the grand finale the live nativity scene with a real baby, of course!

Not only can this be an unforgettable learning experience, it can be a community outreach, too! Other possibilities: Holy Week and the Passion story, Bible times in the streets of Jerusalem, and the Sea of Galilee at a pool or beach.

157

● **Service projects**—Some of the most successful learning adventures take place when people reach out to someone in need. The "adventure factor" increases when students must actually interact with the ones in need—the elderly, the homeless, and poverty-stricken children and their families. You never know what the outcome may be. Sometimes the needy aren't grateful or they don't know how to express their feelings. Sometimes workers realize that the needy are happier than they themselves are!

Getting actively involved in service projects holds the most power when the experiences are intentionally debriefed. You'll lose lots of valuable learning if you don't discuss what's happened, what people are feeling, and how Scripture connects with everything. Reaching out and talking about that experience can be active learning at its best.

● **Classroom adventures**—Many people think adventure happens only beyond classroom walls. That's not so. Here are two unforgettable in-class adventures:

WHO DO YOU TRUST?
(For middle schoolers through adults)

Ask two volunteers to come to the front of the room. Distribute balloons to the rest of the students. Have the students blow up and tie off their balloons. Say: **In a moment, each of you will come up and stand in front of one of the volunteers and face away from him or her. You'll then**

hold your balloon over your head. If you choose the right person, your balloon won't be popped. But if you choose the wrong person, watch out! After each person comes up, I'll tell the volunteers who'll be the "popper" for the next round. Any questions?

Take the volunteers aside and give them each a pin or bent paper clip. Tell one to always pop the balloons and the other to never pop the balloons. Explain that even though you'll take them aside after each person comes up, only the original popper will pop the balloons. Also tell them both to try to convince the rest of the class they won't pop the balloons.

Have the first student come up and choose a volunteer. Then have the student stand facing away from the volunteer and hold his or her balloon above his or her head. Say: **Ready...go!**

Watch the expressions of the students as the balloon is or isn't popped. After each person has had a turn, form a circle.

Ask:

● **What made you choose one person over the other?** (He or she didn't pop any balloons; I avoided the person who always popped the balloons.)

● **How did your trust develop for the person who never popped the balloons?** (The more times he or she told the truth, the more I began to believe him or her; you could rely on each person doing the same thing.)

● **How is this like believing in God?** (You need to believe that God won't hurt you; it's like God is always consistent—he wouldn't lie.)

Say: **Believing in God is like trusting the per-**

son who did what he or she said. If Christianity had come from a God who constantly lied and cheated his people, it'd be difficult to believe in it. But we can trust Christianity partly because we know who it came from—the God who proved himself by taking care of his people in the Old Testament.[9]

DEALING WITH DISABILITIES
(For fifth-graders through adults)

Choose an area in your building as a "safety zone" for this activity. Form teams of four and give each student one slip from the "Airline Injuries" handout on page 162.

Say: **You've been in a plane crash in a remote mountain area. Miraculously, you've all survived, with varying injuries. To win this survival game, three people from your team must make it to the safety zone, moving only as your injuries allow. Anyone who doesn't arrive within two minutes will die because the plane will explode.**

Tell students where the safety zone is and have them hurry to get there. After two minutes, bring the teams together.

Have teams sit in circles on the floor. Tell teams to assign one person to act as a scribe to record their ideas, another to act as a representative, a third to act as a reader, and a fourth to be an encourager who urges everyone to participate in the discussion.

Ask teams to read Leviticus 19:14-16 and discuss the following questions:

● **During this activity, how were people treated differently because of their injuries?** (It was hard to move someone who was paralyzed; we couldn't convince the guy with head injuries to come with us.)

● **How did you feel about the way your team treated you? Explain.** (Good, because we all worked together; disappointed, because I felt left out; frustrated, because I couldn't do much to help my team.)

● **How was this activity like the way we sometimes treat people who have real disabilities?** (We don't know how to act toward them; we tend to leave them out of our activities; we don't expect them to accomplish much.)

● **What attitudes about people with disabilities does Leviticus 19:14-16 present?** (We should treat disabled people with respect; we show respect for God by helping disabled people.)

● **What's difficult about following the instructions in Leviticus 19:14-16?** (I'm uncomfortable around disabled people; I don't want my friends to make fun of me for hanging around people with disabilities; I don't know how a disabled person wants to be treated.)

● **What are the rewards of having an attitude similar to the one described in Leviticus 19:14-16?** (I can make new friends with all kinds of people; my actions can give honor to God; people will treat me like I treat them.)

After a few minutes, end the small group discussions. Have the representatives take turns telling how their teams responded.

AIRLINE INJURIES

Photocopy this handout and cut apart enough slips so each student can have one.

Your left leg is broken. You can't use it at all.

You're paralyzed from the waist down. That means you can't move unless someone carries you or you drag yourself with your arms.

You have a broken right arm and left foot. You can't use either one at all.

You're unable to see.

You're confused and mistrusting due to a head injury. Disagree with everyone. Try to convince your team members that you're right and they're wrong.

Say: **Because God accepts us, we can accept others, regardless of what they can or can't do. Everyone benefits when we put into practice the attitude taught in Leviticus 19:14-16.**[10]

Active learning is an adventure. Whether it's researching and re-creating Bethlehem (instead of hearing a lecture about it), reaching out to people in need (instead of reading about them), popping balloons to show trust (instead of simply studying Scripture about trust), or becoming handicapped (instead of guessing what it might be like to be disabled)—you never know exactly how the adventure will turn out. Adventure possibilities are endless and so is the learning.

FUN AND/OR CAPTIVATING IDEAS

It's too bad so many people think learning is boring. Here are some ideas that will captivate learners and allow them to have fun in the process.

1. Baby care—Help young people experience the responsibility connected with having a baby. Adults can lecture teenagers about the realities of raising a child, but that method pales in comparison to this: Give each young person a five-pound bag of rice. (You could use a raw egg, but some people have found the weight and feel of the bag to be more realistic.)

For one week have teenagers each take care of their bag of rice as if it were a real baby. That means they must name it, clothe it, buy it food

and diapers, and keep it with them at all times unless they arrange for adequate babysitting. If anything happens to the "baby," they'll be brought to
their peers for judgment.

This activity allows students to feel the pressures
of responsibility, embarrassment, hassle, novelty,
pride—all sorts of feelings connected with having
a baby at their age. With proper debriefing, this
activity could result in learning that profoundly
affects young people's decisions concerning premarital sexual activity.

2. The Lord's Supper—Help people understand the history of Jesus' Last Supper with the disciples. Hold a Passover meal with all the special
foods and readings connected with the ceremony.
Let students research the Passover and prepare the
Seder feast. Have them also make the communion
bread. Doing this around Good Friday brings a
deeper meaning to Christ's death on the cross and
the communion celebration.

3. A trial—Set up a judge and jury. Put someone on trial accused of being a Christian. Use
defense and prosecution attorneys. Have students
decide whether there's enough evidence to con-
vict that person of being a Christian.

4. Classroom surprises—Here are two very different classroom activities that will engage learners:

JESUS CALLS ZACCHAEUS

(For preschoolers)

Hold up a clear plastic sandwich bag full of nickels and ask:

- **What do you see in this little bag?**
- **I have to work hard to save my money—how do you think I'd feel if someone took it away from me?**
- **Would you feel bad if you were the person who took it from me?**

Say: **God loves us and never wants us to feel bad, and that's one reason he told us not to steal.**

(Remove the bag of nickels from view so children won't be distracted by it.)

Let me tell you about a man who was grumpy and unhappy because he was stealing people's money. His name was Zacchaeus, and he had lots of money but no friends.

Say "Zacchaeus" with me. *(Children repeat "Zacchaeus.")* Every time you hear the name *Zacchaeus,* I want you to make a grumpy face. Remember, no one liked *Zacchaeus.* Show me your grumpy faces. Everyone knew *Zacchaeus* was stealing their money, and they didn't like to be with him.

One day all the people were running through the town saying, "Jesus is coming! Jesus is coming!" Let's pretend we're the crowd. *(Have the children jump up and point toward the door of the room as they say, "Jesus is coming!")*

The crowd of people lined the road to see Jesus.

Zacchaeus was a short man, and no one would let him peek through the crowd, so what do you think he did? He climbed a tree to get a better look. Let's all pretend we're climbing trees, too. *(Show children how to pretend to climb a tree.)*

Are you all up in your trees?

Sure enough, once *Zacchaeus* got up in that tree, he could see Jesus coming down the road. *Zacchaeus* got so excited he almost fell out of the tree! Jesus and the crowd of people kept coming down the road. When Jesus got to where *Zacchaeus* was, he suddenly stopped and looked up.

"*Zacchaeus*," Jesus said,"come down from that tree. I want to go to your house."

(If you're familiar with the song "Zacchaeus Was a Wee Little Man," teach it to the children at this point in the story.)

Zacchaeus couldn't believe his ears. He was surprised that Jesus knew his name. But do you know what? God knows all of us by name, doesn't he, (name a child)?

Boy, did *Zacchaeus* ever feel special and happy that Jesus wanted to go to his house for dinner! He scrambled down the tree and said, "Oh, yes, Jesus, you're welcome to come to my house."

Now instead of making a grumpy face when you hear the name *Zacchaeus,* smile instead. Because after *Zacchaeus* met Jesus, everything changed.

Zacchaeus promised Jesus that he would give half of his money to poor people so they could buy food and clothes. And he promised Jesus that he would give back all the money he had stolen from people. In fact, he promised to give back *more* money than he had stolen.

Zacchaeus was glad that Jesus was willing to forgive him for stealing. *Zacchaeus* felt clean and happy inside. He was glad that instead of stealing from people, he was helping people. Suddenly *Zacchaeus* had more friends! But his very best friend was Jesus!

Ask:

● **At the beginning of the story, why didn't Zacchaeus have very many friends?**

● **How did Zacchaeus feel when Jesus found him in the tree and asked to come to his house for dinner?**

● **How did Zacchaeus change after he met Jesus?**

● **Why did Zacchaeus' face change from a grumpy face to a happy face?**

Say: Helping people and sharing his money made Zacchaeus happy. It makes me happy, too, so when it's time to leave today, I'll give each of you a nickel from my bag.[11]

THIS LITTLE LIGHT
(For fifth-graders through adults)

Form two teams—team Y and team Z. Have team Y split into two lines, stand six feet apart, and face each other to form a human corridor.

Give team Z one long, lit candle. Have team Z's members take turns walking down team Y's corridor without letting the candle blow out. (Relight the candle as needed.) Tell team Y they can't move

TEACHER TIPS

● Be sure to caution students to handle the candle safely during this activity. You may want to have water or a fire extinguisher nearby in case of an accident.

● If your class is made up of five or fewer students, select one student volunteer to walk down the corridor with the candle. Use the rest of the class to form the corridor. Then have students from the corridor take turns switching places with the volunteer. If your class is larger than 20, form four teams and make two corridors.

or bend toward the candle, but they should try to blow out the candle as many times as they can.

See how many students make it through the corridor with the candle lit. Then have teams switch roles. When all the students have had a turn, collect and extinguish the candle. Form groups of no more than four and have students read Matthew 5:14-16 among themselves. Direct students to number off within their groups from one to four.

Say: **Discuss the next few questions in your groups. Then I'll call out a number from one to four. The person in your group whose number I call will be responsible for sharing an answer from your group with all of us.**

Ask:

● **How did you feel as you tried to keep the candle lit? Explain.** (Frustrated, because I couldn't walk fast enough; happy, because I made it through with my candle burning.)

● **What did you do to keep the candle**

from getting blown out? (I covered it up; I held it over my head; I walked backward.)

● **What do you do when friends, teachers, or others who aren't Christians try to blow out the flame of your faith?** (Tell them how I feel; ask my parents for help; pray for that person.)

● **Why is it hard sometimes to be a light to those people?** (They might not believe in Jesus; teachers might teach things I don't believe.)

● **How can God help you "keep your candle burning" when you face people whose views conflict with your faith?** (God can help me stand for what I believe; God can help me get along with them in spite of our different views.)

● **How can we help each other face people whose views conflict with our faith?** (Remind each other of Matthew 5:14-16; pray for one another.)

Say: **Our faith can help us get along with others, even when their views are different from what we believe. The "light" of our faith can also help others see God's love, so let's do a little exercise to encourage each other in shining our "lights."**

Form a circle and give one student a lit candle. Have students pass the candle around the circle and complete this sentence about the person on their right: "A way I see God shining in you is . . . " Students may say things such as "through your smile," "in your positive attitude," or "by your helpfulness."

Blow out the candle when everyone is finished.[12]

Each example given shows a way to captivate learn-

ers through exciting activities. Imagine the fun of naming a "baby," realizing the connection between the Old Testament Passover and Jesus' sacrifice on the cross, creating a mock trial, hearing and doing the Zacchaeus story, and running a gantlet while keeping your candle lit! Active learning such as this generates interest and excitement. And not only that, it helps students discover and own what they're learning.

TOTAL INVOLVEMENT IDEAS

One of active learning's hallmarks is how it involves everyone. Instead of one-way lectures, here are two classroom activities that illustrate that kind of involvement.

PUZZLED!
(For senior highers)

Form groups of three or four, and give each group a 10- to 15-piece puzzle and a blindfold. Ask a volunteer in each group to be blindfolded and another to dismantle the puzzle. Then have the blindfolded volunteers try to put the puzzles together without any help from the other members of their groups.

After a couple of minutes of frustration, have the volunteers remove their blindfolds.

Ask:

● **How did you feel trying to complete the puzzle while you were blindfolded?** (Frustrated; helpless.)

● **How is trying to plan for your future like putting a puzzle together while you're blindfolded?** (It's hard to know what happens next; you can't see how everything fits together.)

● **When you think about what you want to do in the future, is it easy to see how all the pieces fit together? Why or why not?** (Yes, I'm going to go to college and then get a job; no, I'm confused about what I want to do.)

Have a volunteer read Proverbs 3:5-6 aloud. Then have another person in each group put on a blindfold.

Say: **This time, the members of your group can tell you what to do and even guide your hands, but they can't put any pieces in place themselves.**

When all the puzzles are completed, have the volunteers remove their blindfolds.

Ask:

● **Why was completing the puzzle so much easier this time?** (Because of the help and guidance from the other group members; we weren't so alone.)

Read Proverbs 3:5-6 again. Ask:

● **How is the help you received from your group like the help God offers in these verses?** (We don't have to figure everything out for ourselves; we can trust someone who sees more and knows more than we do.)

● **Who really deserves credit for the puzzle being completed?** (The seeing helpers; the ones who guided me.)

● **Should we trust God completely to put**

the pieces of our future into place? Why or why not? (Yes, God knows what's best; no, we're in charge of our futures.)

● **How do you think God feels when we try to do things on our own, without seeking his wisdom?** (Dismayed; sad.)

Say: **The future is a precious commodity. Only God can see how things will turn out. Still, whether we trust him with our future or blindly try to put it together ourselves is a choice God leaves to us.**[13]

SUPPORT NET
(For senior highers through adults)

Place a bunch of 3×5 cards and pencils on the floor in the center of the circle. Say: **We all have aspects of our faith such as patience, love for others, and trust in God that can help us deal with ridicule. Think of the person on your left and what his or her strengths are. Then pick up a card and a pencil, and write on the card one strength you see in the person on your left. Give that card to that person to read. Then write at least one more card for someone else in the circle.**

When students each have at least one card, tell them to place the cards next to each other on the floor in the center of the circle. Then have students help you tape the cards together to form a "net." Have everyone huddle together and hold the net in the center of the circle.

Say: **By supporting each other with encour-**

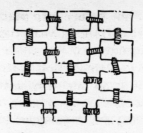

agement, we form a net that can help us feel confident in our faith.

While still holding the net, have volunteers close in prayer thanking God for the person on their right for the gift of support he or she gives. Conclude by asking God to use your group's strengths as a net to help face good and bad times.[14]

By involving everyone, learners can't sit by while someone else does the "work" of learning. Each person will learn by doing. When everyone's engaged through experiences such as the puzzle and building a net, concepts will make a lot more sense.

DEBRIEFING IDEAS

Without the debriefing step, experiences may result in little learning. Try these ideas and see how discussing them can help push learners to action.

1. Mission investigation—Have class members collect a variety of mission organizations' addresses and write them for information. Ask for financial statements and a breakdown of how money is allocated. Allow students to analyze which organizations would spend their money in a way the class feels good about. Then have students pledge to support the mission organization of their choice for a year.

This activity's strength lies in the debriefing. Students must discuss and wrestle with facts and information concerning the organization.

The debriefing and choosing will result in long-term learning and values.

Classes may also write congressional representatives, protest trashy TV programs, or find out more about your denomination. The information isn't the end of the investigation; the debriefing is what helps people explore issues, feelings, and actions to take.

2. Congregational survey—Have classes choose a topic they'd like to explore and devise questions to uncover information. For example, teenagers might want to find out how adults view music in the church. They could ask, "What would you say if our church used more contemporary music? (a) I'd strongly oppose it, (b) It doesn't matter, (c) I'd support it and think it's great!" Or find out from church members, "What must a person do to be saved?"

Gathering the information isn't the end. Use the information as a springboard for discussion. Ask, "What did you learn? How do you feel about what you learned? What surprised you about what you learned? What action might you take because of what you learned?" Debrief your findings.

3. Classroom activities—See how the following activity uses debriefing to help students learn about sin and forgiveness.

THE WEIGHT OF SIN
(For middle schoolers through adults)

Give students each a large Bible or another large book such as a dictionary. Ask them to keep their elbows straight and hold the books in front of them at shoulder height. Tell students each to hold the book there as long as they can.

As they are holding their books, have students talk about times they messed up in a relationship and how they felt. Periodically, ask students how their arms feel.

Ask:

● **How difficult was it to hold the weight up?** (At first it was easy; it got tougher as time went on.)

● **How did you feel as the book began to feel heavier?** (Sore; nervous; frustrated.)

● **How is this like the way you feel when you've done something wrong against someone and you haven't asked forgiveness for your actions?** (I feel worse by the minute when I don't resolve problems; I begin to feel bad about the times I've messed up.)

● **How did you feel when you were able to put the book down?** (I felt relieved; I felt good.)

● **How is this like the way you feel when you've been forgiven for something you did against someone?** (It's like a heavy weight that you have to hold up has been lifted; it feels so good when the burden of sin is taken away.)

Say: **When we mess up and do things we know aren't right, we begin to feel the weight**

of sin weighing us down. Fortunately, our sins can be forgiven so we can move on with our lives and feel good about ourselves again.

Next give students each a Bible. Say: **Jesus met a woman who was experiencing exactly the kind of weight we've been talking about.** Have a volunteer read aloud John 8:2-5. Ask students to imagine the woman standing in the middle of all those people.

Ask:

● **How do you think the woman in this passage felt?** (Scared; embarrassed; ashamed.)

Have a volunteer stand so the rest of the students can see him or her. Give the volunteer several books to hold. Explain that those books represent the weight of the volunteer's own sin. Then have students each come up and hand the volunteer another book. Explain that each of their books will represent the condemnation of that person.

Ask the volunteer:

● **How do you feel with all of those burdens?** (Weighed down; sad; frustrated.)

Ask the rest of the class:

● **When have you felt like our volunteer?** (When things have been going badly; when I've messed up too many times.)

Have the volunteer set the books down, then read aloud John 8:6-11.

Ask:

● **Why do you think Jesus began writing in the dirt?** (To focus attention away from the woman; to show the Pharisees he wasn't going to answer the way they wanted him to.)

Say: **Jesus told the Pharisees, "Anyone here who has never sinned can throw the first stone at her." That got them thinking—and leaving.**

Ask:

● **What can we learn from Jesus' response to the Pharisees?** (We shouldn't condemn others; we're all sinners.)

● **How do you think the woman felt after this experience?** (Relieved; grateful; hopeful; clean.)

● **What can we learn from Jesus' response to the woman?** (Jesus will forgive us; Jesus wants to make us different.)

Have students read 1 John 1:8–2:2 silently. As they read, randomly write the following words on a chalkboard or a sheet of newsprint: "drunkenness," "premarital sex," "theft," "selfishness," "lying," "cheating," and "profanity."

After a few minutes, have students look at the list. Ask students to think about things they've done that've separated them from God. Then say: **We're all guilty of sin. But when we confess our sins to God, he forgives us and completely cleanses our lives.** Erase the chalkboard or tear down the paper and throw it in a trash can.

Say: **It wasn't easy for God to forgive our sins. Because God is righteous, he couldn't just overlook our sins or pretend they didn't happen.** Ask students to open their Bibles to Hebrews 9:22. Have a volunteer read the verse aloud. Explain that in the Old Testament, people were instructed to sacrifice animals as a way to repent of their sins. The sacrifices were not perfect and had to be done again and again.

Have another student read aloud Hebrews 9:27-28. Ask:

● **What does this passage tell us about forgiveness?** (Jesus died for our sins; Jesus was the sacrifice to take away all our sins.)[15]

Debriefing is a key to successful active learning. Unless you discuss the information gathered from the mission organizations or congregational surveys, the information stands alone. When students actively converse with one another about topics, they learn from each other. They also learn how to articulate thoughts and feelings. Classrooms flourish with sessions such as "The Weight of Sin." It's in these debriefing times that students unravel issues of faith by talking about them together.

7 USE INTERACTIVE LEARNING

So far we've explored several bad habits we church people picked up from our own schooling. We've looked at

- the forgotten goals of education;

- a misguided focus on teaching instead of learning;

- an obsession with the unimportant;

- cramming for coverage rather than digging for thoroughness;

- the fouled priority of memorization over understanding;

- a penchant for the time wasters of r-bbits, fill-in-the-blanks, and word jumbles;

- the lack of thinking; and

- a lopsided preference for passive learning—lectures and textbooks.

Well, we're not done yet. From kindergarten to college and seminary, the hidden curriculum has ingrained in us still more bad habits.

So, what other baggage did we pick up from our own schooling? We've been programmed to believe that individualism and competitiveness are the superior structures for learning. Little desks, separated from one another, placed in neat rows, all facing one direction. The bell curve—a grading system that, by its nature, requires that a certain number fail. The worship of individual effort—working alone—and the simultaneous discouraging of teamwork. The separation of the "slow learners" from the "gifted students."

And we wonder why American schools trail the rest of the industrialized world?

"Asian elementary schools are not highly competitive. Children are eager to display what they know, and they are challenged to learn what is being taught rather than to surpass other children. One of the secrets of Asian schooling is the strong identification pupils feel with each other and with the school."

—Harold Stevenson and James Stigler,
The Learning Gap[1]

Over the course of many years American schools teach that working in isolation is the way to learn, the way to work. Then when people leave school and enter the work force they discover that real life requires a lot more teamwork than they were taught.

"Most people don't have trouble at work because of lack of skills. They have trouble because they haven't learned to get along with others," says Susan Sprague, a school administrator in Mesa, Arizona. She directs an innovative curriculum that emphasizes student interaction, cooperation, and active learning. It's regarded as the best districtwide science program in the United States.

In those classrooms, and in an increasing number of classrooms throughout America, student desks no longer form neat rows. They're clumped in bunches. They face each other in threes or fours. Students work together to achieve common goals (just like most of us do in real life). They help one another, encourage one another, teach one another.

Everyone knows that the person who learns the most in any class is the teacher. Explaining a concept to someone else is usually more helpful to the explainer than the listener. So why not let the students do more teaching? That's one of the chief benefits of *interactive learning*. But that's a tough idea to sell to teachers who've always done it the old way. Educators estimate that 93 percent of teaching consists of direct commands from the teacher to the student.[2] Educator John Goodlad said in *A Place Called School* that only 5 percent of class time is typically spent in discussion.[3]

WHAT IS INTERACTIVE LEARNING?

As we saw in the last chapter, active learning revolves around an experience. *Interactive learning* occurs when students discuss and work cooperatively in pairs or small groups.

Interactive learning encourages learners to work together. It honors the fact that students can learn from one another—not just from the teacher or the text.

Let's look at a simple example. In an old-style scenario, the teacher lectures and poses questions to the class. One or two students raise their hands and reward the teacher with the "right" answer. But in an interactive classroom, the teacher poses the question, then asks students to discuss the question in pairs or foursomes. *Every* individual is involved. Everybody works on problem solving. Every person learns.

Interactive learning differs from individual and competitive models. Here's a sketch of each structure:

INDIVIDUAL: "I do my own thing."

Students work and respond alone. They strive for their own individual success. One student's success does not benefit others. Achievement of each student's learning goals is unrelated to what other students do. (Think of Sunday school student books and work sheets.)

COMPETITIVE: "I win; you lose."

Students work and respond alone, and they strive to be better than their classmates. One student's success is another's failure. Students work against each other to obtain a goal only one or a few achieve. (Think of Bible quizzing and memorization contests.)

THREE LEARNING STRUCTURES

INDIVIDUAL   COMPETITIVE   INTERACTIVE

INTERACTIVE: "We sink or swim together."

Students work together, in pairs or small groups, to accomplish shared goals. They teach one another and learn from one another. Success as a group is celebrated. Positive interdependence promotes individual and group learning.

In short, interactive learning views fellow students as resources in the learning process. The individual and competitive systems view fellow students as irrelevant or adversarial.

> **"Two people are better than one,**
> **because they get more done by working**
> **together. If one falls down, the other**
> **can help him up. But it is bad for the**
> **person who is alone and falls, because**
> **no one is there to help."**
>
> *—Ecclesiastes 4:9-10*

CHARACTERISTICS OF INTERACTIVE LEARNING

Helping one another learn enhances all students' levels of learning and dramatically boosts retention. Interactive learning not only helps people learn, but it also helps learners feel better about themselves and get along better with others. It accomplishes these things better than the independent or competitive method.

Why does interactive learning work so well? Let's

183

examine six characteristics.

1. INTERACTIVE LEARNING IS STUDENT-BASED, NOT TEACHER-BASED.

The focus is on the learner rather than the teacher. Students work—and learn—in pairs and small groups. The room is often filled with learning noise.

Make no mistake. Student-based learning is a real departure for most teachers. Veteran educator and author Jane Healy visited many schools to study children's use of language. "I had trouble finding anything but isolated phrases or short answers to teachers' questions," she said. "Much of the 'talk' was a one-way street, as the teacher presented the material, gave directions, or asked factual questions requiring only brief answers. Rarely were children encouraged to talk to each other, ask each other questions—or even, in fact, to ask questions at all!"[4]

Interactive learning depends on students working together to make discoveries rather than teachers imparting all the facts and ideas. Learning moves at the students' pace. Though students may cover less teacher-chosen material, they'll usually learn more, in greater depth.

Teachers don't have to have all the answers. In fact, they learn right along with the students.

2. INTERACTIVE LEARNING PROMOTES POSITIVE INTERDEPENDENCE.

Interactive students need each other. They may problem-solve together, or read the Bible together, or share their insights together.

This interdependence is a picture of what Paul describes in his letter to the Corinthians: "So then there are many parts, but only one body. The eye cannot say to the hand, 'I

184

don't need you..."' (1 Corinthians 12:12-31).

People in interactive-learning groups soon learn the wisdom of Paul's words. They learn from one another.

Try to work the following problem alone. Look at the letters on both sides of the "fence" below. See if you can figure out the system that's used to place the letters on the left or right side of the fence. Where would the rest of the alphabet go?

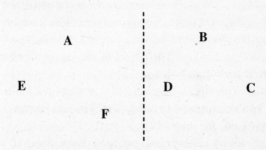

Can you figure it out? If not, grab a friend and see if the two of you can solve the puzzle.

Most people have trouble solving this problem by themselves. But the chances of solving it improve considerably when two or three or four work together on the problem. The Ecclesiastes quote applies: "Two people are better than one."

(The solution is quite simple. If you were seeking some complex mathematical formula, you didn't get it. If you had an intuitive person in your interactive group, you may have cracked it. The left side of the fence is reserved for letters with straight lines. Letters with curved lines go on the right side of the fence.)

The point is: Interdependent pairs or small groups can usually solve problems faster and learn more than individuals working alone.

3. INTERACTIVE LEARNING ALLOWS STUDENTS TO DISCOVER.

Learners find answers rather than passively receiving them from the teacher. They work together to successfully complete their learning expeditions.

Take a look at this interactive excerpt from Group's Active Bible Curriculum® on the Ten Commandments:

Form two teams. Have teams gather at one end of the room and place a piece of masking tape across the other end of the room. Give each team three balloons, a pail, and two spoons. Say: **The object of this game is to be the first team finished. Go!**

When kids start asking what they're supposed to do, say: **You're supposed to finish first. The rest you have to figure out for yourselves.**

Let kids try to play the game. Stop it after about five minutes.

Say: **What I wanted you to do was to have two people use the spoons to carry a balloon down to the tape and back without touching the balloon with their hands, then deposit the balloon in the pail and give the spoons to the next pair, who would take the next balloon. The first team with all three balloons in or on the pail would have won.**

An associate of ours recently did this activity with a group of middle schoolers. The kids were duly frustrated and bewildered. During the debriefing, the teams discovered the message. "Oh, I get it," one kid said. "We didn't have any rules, and the game didn't work. That's why we need rules—like the Ten Commandments—isn't it?"

The teacher could have simply told them that message

in a much shorter period of time. But the team experience allowed the kids to discover the truth about God's commandments. They learned. And they'll remember.

4. INTERACTIVE LEARNING LEAVES NO ONE OUT.

In interactive learning, everyone responds, not just one or two talkative students.

In independent and competitive learning models, many if not most students' minds wander. They're accountable only to the teacher. And they typically outnumber the teacher by a large ratio. The teacher can call on only one student at a time. Chances are excellent the teacher will not interact with most of the students most of the time. They know it. And they mentally check out.

But in interactive learning, each pair or team is responsible for responding. Partners count on each other—and hold each other accountable.

Interactive teachers know how to capitalize on this. They may say, "Stand when you know your partner knows the answer." That motivates everyone to learn.

5. INTERACTIVE LEARNING BUILDS INTERPERSONAL SKILLS.

When students work together to reach common goals, they learn more than the subject matter at hand. They learn how to get along with one another.

Many people complain that today's younger generation often lacks basic social skills. Some blame the erosion of family communication for this problem. And college graduates reported in a survey that the teamwork skills they now require in adult life were virtually ignored in their schooling.[5] If our young people aren't acquiring people skills elsewhere, the church is a wonderful place for this training.

And interactive learning really delivers this basic interpersonal training. Participants learn communication skills—speaking and listening, decision-making skills, trust, conflict management, negotiation, leadership, and teamwork.

6. INTERACTIVE LEARNING BUILDS RELATIONSHIPS.

In addition to providing lifelong skills, interactive learning promotes relationships among our people. They become friends. One of the real hungers that people of all ages feel when they enter our church doors is the need for relationships. The number one reason teenagers attend a youth group is to make and be with friends. Our high-tech world has produced an epidemic of loneliness.

Why can't the church serve its flock by providing experiences that allow people to interact, to get to know one another?

But no. Most curricula and most teachers speed right past all opportunities to build Christian friendships. Most adult classes we've attended are dominated by a fact-gushing teacher and two or three chatty persons. We could attend for weeks or years without ever saying a word, meeting another person, or contributing to the class.

But interactive learning makes it easy—even for shy people—to talk with others and build relationships. When the leader or teacher asks people to work in pairs or small groups they no longer feel like they're performing in front of a crowd. They're working with a few friends to find solutions to life's questions.

And they're making good Christian friends in the

process. And it's those friendships—more than any formal teaching—that may keep them coming to church in the future.

We can't afford not to use interactive learning in the church.

INTERACTIVE-LEARNING TECHNIQUES

Here's a selection of interactive-learning techniques that work well in the church. With any of these models, teachers may assign students to specific partners or small groups. This will maximize cooperation and learning by preventing all the rowdies from linking up. And it will allow for new friendships to form outside of established cliques.

Following any period of partner or small group work, the teacher may reconvene the entire class for large group processing. During this time the teacher may ask for reports or discoveries from individuals or teams. This technique builds in accountability for the teacherless pairs and small groups.

PAIR-SHARE

With this technique students turn to a partner and respond to a question or problem from the teacher or leader. Every learner responds. There are no passive observers. The teacher may then ask people to tell their partners' responses.

This requires students to talk as well as listen. Talking cements concepts and enhances the chances of those concepts being transferred to life outside the church walls.

"Good learning arrives
out of dialogue."

—Ted Sizer

This technique is so simple to do—and so effective. But the church has virtually ignored it. How often do you see language in your church curriculum materials such as this: "Turn to a partner and answer this question…"? How often do you see church teachers or preachers allowing pairs to answer questions?

No, the overwhelming practice in the church is for the teacher to solicit answers from the class or group as a whole. Typically one or two vocal people talk. The rest allow their minds to wander to more interesting thoughts. This picture is true in adult classes as well as children's and youth classes.

Pair-shares work with all ages. Many teachers would never imagine asking kindergartners to share in pairs. But it works! Instead of asking the whole class, "Can anyone here think of a time you've helped someone?" say, "Please turn to the person beside you and tell about a time you helped somebody." Even 5-year-olds learn more when they each have a chance to talk and become involved.

READING BUDDIES

In lower grades, students read passages or stories to a partner, getting any needed help with words or meaning. With upper grades and adults, students react to material with their partners.

Again, most curriculum and most teachers call for the Scripture passage to be read to the whole class by one person. One reads; the others doze.

Why not relinquish some teacher control and let partners

read and react? They'll all be involved—and learn more.

Teachers may fear that some partners—without direct teacher surveillance—may not concentrate on the passage. Believe us; they're not concentrating now under the teacher-directed model. We have nothing to lose by trying the buddy system for some of our learning.

LEARNING GROUPS

Students read passages or stories together in small groups and answer questions. Each person in the learning group may be assigned a specific role. Some examples:

- reader
- recorder (makes notes of key thoughts expressed during the reading or discussion)
- checker (makes sure everyone understands and agrees with answers arrived at by the group)
- encourager (urges silent members to share their thoughts)

When everyone has a specific responsibility, knows what it is, and contributes to a small group, much is accomplished and much is learned.

SUMMARY PARTNERS

One student reads a paragraph, then the partner summarizes the paragraph or interprets its meaning. Partners alternate roles with each paragraph.

The paraphrasing technique also works well in discussions. Anyone who wishes to share a thought must first paraphrase what the previous person just said. This sharpens listening skills and demonstrates the power of feedback communication.

JIGSAW

Each person in a small group learns a different concept, Scripture, or part of an issue. Then each teaches the others in the group. Thus, all members teach and all must learn the others' discoveries. This technique is called a jigsaw because individuals are responsible to their groups for different pieces of the puzzle.

Here's a sample of a jigsaw:

Assign four-person teams. Have the members of each team number off from one to four. Have all the ones go to one corner of the room, all the twos to another corner, and so on.

Tell team members they're responsible for learning information in their numbered corners and then teaching their team members when they return to their original teams.

Give the following assignments to various corners:

Corner one: Read Psalm 22. Discuss (among all the ones) and list the prophecies made about Jesus.

Corner two: Read Isaiah 52:13–53:12. Discuss and list the prophecies made about Jesus.

Corner three: Read Matthew 27:1-32. Discuss and list the things that happened to Jesus.

Corner four: Read Matthew 27:33-66. Discuss and list the things that happened to Jesus.

After the corner groups have met and discussed, have all learners return to their original teams and report what they've learned. Then have each team determine which prophecies about Jesus were fulfilled in the passages from Matthew.

Call on various individuals in each team to report one or two prophecies that were fulfilled.

ORIENTING INTERACTIVE LEARNERS

Don't expect students to immediately adapt and succeed in interactive groups. Remember their frame of reference. They're accustomed to individual and competitive learning situations. They're not used to cooperating, serving one another, talking with one another. We can't expect them to instantly feel comfortable in this new and foreign learning environment.

So don't give up after the first few attempts at interactive learning. Understand that, like most new skills, this one will take a little practice.

Let your people know you're trying some new approaches to learning. Assure them that, though they may feel uncomfortable at first, they'll grow to enjoy the interaction.

Also spend time educating your learners about some interactive-learning procedural signals. Because you'll be constantly shifting from large group instruction to small group work, the noise levels will rise. In order to easily regain everyone's attention everyone needs to know the signal. We don't recommend "Shhhhhhhhh!" or "Everybody shut up!" Instead, train everyone to watch or listen for a signal such as

● switching the lights off and on,

● blowing a whistle,

● raising one hand—prompting others to raise a hand and become quiet,

● a rhythmic hand clap, or

● a toot on a harmonica.

Soon your students will learn the culture of interactive learning. And they'll be on their way to significant spiritual growth.

The "DO IT" section that follows offers practical programming ideas to help you share and apply these principles in your church.

Now that you realize the benefits of interactive learning, it's time to try it. Here are a number of experiences for different age levels that exemplify interactive-learning techniques. Here goes!

USING PAIR-SHARES

The following activity shows the value of partners working together and learning from one another.

MAKING THE WORD COME ALIVE
(For youth and adults)

Have students pair up and put on blindfolds. Say: **I'm going to give each of you an item to describe to your partner. When I give the item to you, beginning with the person who has the longest name, describe your object without naming it or saying what it's used for. You may or may not know what the item is, and that's okay. You'll each have about 20 seconds to describe your item to your partner. Listeners, make a mental snapshot of what you think the described item looks and feels like. Then take it from your partner to touch for yourself.**

Give each person an item from a box of miscellaneous items. Your box might include paper clips, key rings, bottle caps, or other, more obscure items such as parts from toasters, stereos, or other mechanical items. Just bring in your junk drawer from home!

After partners have described and exchanged their items, have students remove their blindfolds. Have them tell their partners:

● **How did you feel as you tried to describe the item you were holding?** (Frustrated; confident; unsure.)

● **How did your mental picture of each item change when you got to hold the item?** (I discovered what was being described; I understood better.)

● **How did your image of each item change after you got to actually see it?** (I knew what it was all along; I understood what my partner was trying to communicate.)

Have partners report back to the whole group. Then have partners read aloud John 1:1-18. Encourage them to alternate reading verses. After each verse is read, have the listening partner summarize what he or she thinks that verse means.

Then have partners discuss:

● **How is what God did by becoming flesh like what you did when you held the items from our last activity in your hands?** (God became someone we could better understand; God became flesh so we could relate to him.)

● **Why did God decide to come to earth as Jesus?** (So we could know him better; so he wouldn't be so intangible.)

Have partners tell the group their discoveries. Then form a circle and have people place the items from the activity in the center of the circle. Have students in turn choose one item from the pile and explain how it represents something about Jesus as human or divine. For example, someone who picks up a pencil might say, "If Jesus walked the earth today, he could actually use this pencil," or "Jesus has the power to create the tree that this pencil was made from, but he chose to walk among the trees with us." Encourage creativity in their descriptions of Jesus.

Say: **As we explore what the Bible says about Jesus, we may discover more questions than answers. Don't be afraid to ask your questions and dig deeper. The more we learn about Jesus, the more we'll want to know.**

Give each student a pencil and a sheet of paper. Have students tear their papers into a question mark shape. Say: **On your question mark, write your name, then complete the following sentences:**

● **If Jesus is truly God and truly man, that means I . . .**

● **A question that I still have about Jesus is . . .**

● **One thing I can do to get to know Jesus better is . . .**

Have everyone find new partners and tell one another what they wrote on their question marks.

Join hands in a circle and have partners each say one thing they appreciate about what their partners wrote. For example, someone might say, "I really like the question Brett came up with about Jesus," or "Your idea on how to get to know Jesus better is a good one."

When all have finished, tape the question marks on the wall and leave them up for the rest of the class.[6]

Pair-shares work well in this activity because the technique gives each person a chance to guess and express something about an object. No one can passively sit back. The twosomes allow for less threatening discussions. It's easier to open up and tell one person about your faith questions than it is to tell the whole class. If you would've done this activity in a large group, only one or two bold students probably would've gotten involved. The others could've checked out without learning anything.

The idea of pair-shares can be adapted to almost any classroom setting to enhance involvement.

USING LEARNING GROUPS

Note how the next activity assigns each small-group participant a specific role. This gives each person a job that's important to the group's success.

HIDDEN MESSAGES
(For fifth-graders through adults)

Write the words, "I didn't say you were ugly," on a sheet of newsprint and hang it in front of the class.

Form groups of four. Assign the following roles within each group: one person to act as a scribe to record ideas, another to act as a representative, a third to act as a director, and a fourth to act as an encourager who urges everyone to participate.

Give the scribe for each group a pencil and a sheet of paper. Instruct students to start with the directors and take turns saying the sentence written on the newsprint aloud in their groups, each time strongly emphasizing the next word in the sentence. For example, the director will say, "*I* didn't say you were ugly." The person on the director's right will emphasize "didn't," and so on.

Each time the sentence is read, have the director ask the rest of the group members what the sentence means with this emphasis. Have the scribe write down the group's responses.

When everyone is finished, have groups discuss these questions:

● **How many meanings does this sentence have?** (At least seven.)

● **What interpretations did you come up with?** (I only *thought* you were ugly; someone *else* thought you were ugly.)

● **What, besides words, tells others what you really mean?** (Tone of voice; facial expressions; body language.)

● **How do you respond when your family members at home misinterpret what you say?** (I ignore it; I try to explain myself; I get frustrated and give up.)

Invite the representatives to take turns sharing their groups' answers by referring to the scribe's notes. Next have the director in each group read Ephesians 4:29-32 aloud. Have groups discuss these questions among themselves.

Ask:

● **How would you summarize this passage in seven words or less?** (Use words to help others; be kind and loving.)

● **What causes words to be misinterpreted in our families?** (Mistrust; bad attitudes; not listening.)

● **How can we be sure our family members are hearing the good things we try to communicate?** (Repeatedly say good things to our family members; let our actions match our words; ask for feedback to make sure they've understood what we've said.)

Say: **Sometimes we really do use mean words to hurt our family members. Other times, the words aren't so mean; it's just the way we say them that hurts. Caring communication builds strong families. This means we need to make our communication kind and loving and watch to make sure our words aren't misinterpreted.**[7]

Imagine how this activity works as each person has a special assignment. Learning groups such as this allow every person to make a valuable contribution. It helps boost self-esteem, gives people practice in roles they might not naturally take on, and enhances involvement. The group is counting on each person to do his or her part—group members can't check out.

USING SUMMARY PARTNERS

Watch how the next activity lets students help one another by summarizing and interpreting Scripture for the task at hand.

JUMPING PSALMS

(For children, second-graders and up)

Have kids pair up. Give each pair a Bible, paper, and a pencil. Assign each pair one of these Bible passages: Psalm 8:1-2; Psalm 18:2-3; Psalm 66:3-4; Psalm 149:1 and 3; Psalm 150:1-2. Alternate by having each partner read a verse, followed by the other person paraphrasing that verse. Then have each pair rewrite its psalm into a jump-rope jingle.

Have each pair hold the jump-rope and perform their jingle for the others as the other children jump rope to the rhythm. Take turns until you've heard all the jingles. Encourage kids to remember their jingles and use them on the playground.

After applauding everyone's efforts, ask: **Why is it good to praise God? How can we praise God? What's something about God you like to praise?**

Have children kneel in a circle. Have pairs read aloud their jingles in turn as a closing prayer. After everyone has read, say: **In Jesus' name, amen.**[8]

Just picture children working together in twos to create their jump-rope jingles. Using summary partners allows students to help one another dig into Scripture. In contrast, typical classrooms have only the teacher giving input to the class as a whole. Summary partners increase involvement, belief in the students' abilities, and discovery learning.

USING JIGSAWS

The following activities show how the jigsaw technique can be used. It's an innovative way to show interdependence and the need for each other.

CREATION REVISITED

(For upper-elementary children through middle schoolers)

Form seven groups. A group can be one person. If you have fewer than seven students, combine some of the Scripture passages. Assign each group one of the following passages from Genesis 1: verses 1-5, verses 6-8, verses 9-13, verses 14-19, verses 20-23, verses 24-25, and verses 26-31.

Say: **Read through your verses and decide how you can dramatize them with sound effects and actions. Imagine what it would have been like to be an observer as the earth and sky were formed. You'll have three minutes to prepare; then we'll perform Genesis 1.**

After three minutes, signal everyone to come together.

Say: **Now I'll read Genesis 1 as you perform. Whenever I get to the words "Then God said," I'll point to you and have you all say it with me. Let's practice it once.** Point and say: **Then God said.** Then say: **Great! Here we go with Genesis 1.**

After kids have performed their Scripture verses, compliment them on their effort and creativity.

Then ask:

● **How did you feel as you read and drama-tized this story?** (It reminded me of how great God is; it was hard to imagine how God did all this.)

● **How would you answer someone who says all this happened by chance—that God didn't have anything to do with it?** (I'd say that nothing this complex could happen by chance; I'd say that the first words of the Bible are "In the begin-ning God created," and that's what I believe.)

Say: **It's a privilege to live in God's amaz-ing world. It's hard to believe that anyone could say all this just happened. We can trust the Bible when it says, "In the begin-ning *God created*"!** [9]

By assigning different groups different verses from Scripture, everyone's input is necessary to get the whole story. Just like puzzle pieces, each group's part is vital to complete the Creation picture. Unlike when the teacher or one volunteer reads the Scripture for the class, everyone gets in on the act, increasing involvement and retention.

Here's another twist on the jigsaw approach:

PAL POWER
(For fifth-graders and older)

Form trios. Tell each trio to pick one person to be a lion, one to be a tiger, and one to be a bear (oh my!). Beginning with the lions, have students tell each other about a time someone comforted them when they lost someone or something close to them. For example, the death of a loved one or a pet or a hardship in their families. Make sure the tigers and bears listen carefully for ways to help someone feel better in tough times. Give tigers and bears a chance to tell their examples, too.

Give each student a 3×5 card and a pencil and send the lions to the back of the room. Have the lions read 2 Corinthians 1:3-4 and rewrite it in their own words, with the help of the other lions. Send the tigers to the side of the room to do the same thing with Romans 5:21, and the bears to the front to work on 1 Thessalonians 4:13-18.

After a few minutes give a signal to regain the students' attention. Have students re-form their trios and take turns sharing their rewritten Scriptures. Then, with these Scriptures in mind, have the trios brainstorm things they could do to comfort a friend who's lost a loved one. Have trios write their ideas on the back of one of their 3×5 cards.

Ask the trios:

● **What keeps us from acting on these ideas when we see a friend grieving?** (We don't know what to say; we're not sure if we're wanted; we're uncomfortable talking about death.)

● **Which of the ideas would give you the most comfort?** (I'd like it if someone sent me a card; I'd like to get a hug.)

Say: **These are great ideas to help us comfort a friend who has lost a loved one. We're sometimes tempted to avoid people who are grieving, but Jesus can give us the strength we need to deal with death and grief. He often will use us and our ideas to do just that.**

204

Have trio members each share a tough time they're struggling with right now. After each person shares, have the other two students offer support and encouragement using ideas from Scripture.[10]

Again, the jigsaw technique brings students together to share different pieces of information. In this activity, the students not only provide different portions of Scripture, they also provide support for one another.

8 USE A CURRICULUM THAT PRODUCES AUTHENTIC LEARNING

In previous chapters you've seen what works and what doesn't in helping today's people learn. We've focused on *how* people learn. We've not mentioned much about who does the teaching.

What about the teachers? Many folks will tell you it's the "people, not the program" that cause students to learn and grow. There's some truth to this statement. When most adults think back to their childhood years in Sunday school and youth groups, they more often recall a person, a teacher, than a specific lesson. The Holy Spirit often speaks through God's gifted teachers.

Much has already been written in other works about the importance of teachers showering their students with love, compassion, understanding, encouragement, mentoring, and time outside of church. Since that field has been tilled many times, we won't discuss that aspect in these pages.

Besides, the preponderance of evidence suggests that learning in the church hasn't collapsed because of un-loving, uncompassionate, cold, detached teachers. Nothing in our research or anyone else's indicates that this is the problem.

No, most of our teachers are good people who care about their students. They are volunteers who donate their valuable time because they want to make a difference in others' lives. They, for the most part, do the best they can with the resources they've been given.

So now we turn our attention to what they've been given—the curriculum materials. Most churches dedicate a significant portion of their budgets to printed curriculum materials for all ages. Year in and year out the faithful in the pews deposit their tithes in the plate, trusting the church's purse keepers to use their money wisely. Well, are the big dollars spent on printed curriculum an example of good stewardship? Are we getting our money's worth? Does most of this stuff really bring us closer to our big goals for Christian education? Or is it mostly expensive busywork that closely resembles the stuff our secular schools are just now discovering doesn't work?

> **"There's nothing a human being resents more than busywork. And that's why, frankly, most Sunday school quarterlies could be used more profitably as kindling in your fireplace."**
>
> —*Howard Hendricks,*
> *The 7 Laws of the Teacher* [1]

To help you see a snapshot of what churches are teaching, we perused curricula produced by all major (and most of the minor) publishers—both denominational and independent. We've selected examples to show you a representation of what comprises most Christian curricula. We did not search out extreme, isolated cases. What you'll see in the pages that follow is the norm.

MAJORING IN MINUTIAE

We found piles of student books filled with closed-ended questions looking for factoid answers. Here's one that focuses on the Apostle Paul:

Place of birth (Acts 22:3): _____
List of hardships (2 Corinthians 11:21b-28):
  Number of beatings from Jews: _____
  Number of beatings with rods: _____
  Number of stonings: _____
  Number of shipwrecks: _____
  Time spent in the sea: _____

Here's another that features the story of Noah. The object is to identify what each number relates to in the story.

3	_____
40	_____
450	_____
2	_____
75	_____
7	_____
600	_____
45	_____
150	_____
601	_____
8	_____
25	_____

Numbers are popular, we found. Here's another example that leads the more mathematical third- and fourth-graders to Abraham's and Sarah's ages when their son was born.

The largest number on a clock face is	_____
The number that comes before 20 is	+ _____
	= _____
The number of pennies that equals 2 quarters is	+ _____
	= _____
The number that comes next (5, 6, 7, 8,____) is	+ _____
Sarah's age	= _____
The number of wheels on 5 bicycles is	+ _____
Abraham's age =	_____

If you wanted to determine a Bible character's age, is this how you'd go about it? Is this type of activity the best use of students' time? Are students likely to remember this information? For how long? Will they learn life-changing concepts?

NO-BRAINERS

Many exercises require very little thought—but they do eat up class time. Here's a typical example that beckons students to fill in the missing words that appear in Hosea 11:1-4. Students transfer the missing words from the Revised Standard Version.

When Israel was a _____,
I _____ him . . .
It was I who _____ Ephraim

**(Israel) to _____, I _____
them up in my _____; but they did not
know that I _____ them.**

This particular exercise went on considerably longer
than shown here. It then turned around and required students to repeat the same exercise, same passage, from
another translation. Is transcribing word for word the
best use of students' time?

We ran across the following material in a curriculum for
high schoolers. The teachers guide asks the teacher to show
the class a piece of cheese, then ask these questions:

1. **Where does cheese come from?**
2. **What color could the cow have been that gave
   milk for the cheese?**
3. **What color was the milk?**

What do you suppose those high schoolers are thinking by this point in the interrogation? This study tried to
link nature's mysteries to the mysteries in Revelation.
The real mystery is: Why would anyone ask high
schoolers questions like these?

Dead-end questions aren't limited to children's and
youth material. Here's a sample question from an adult
curriculum:

**In whose home did Jesus make severe charges
against the Pharisees (Luke 11:37)?**

Multiple-choice questions are another favorite time
killer. Here's an example from a third- and fourth-grade
study on Genesis:

What did Noah build after he got off the ark?
 a. castle
 b. restaurant
 c. altar

The same curriculum later asked students to look up Genesis 22:9 and answer this question:

Abraham built an _____.

Is it the students' fault they're bored in church? Do we need any more evidence for why most children and youth say their churches do not cause them to think?

OBSCURING THE OBVIOUS

Some curriculum producers take a perfectly clear piece of God's Word and make it baffling, befuddling, and bewildering. They've been quite creative in this endeavor, we must admit. Every imaginable method for obscuring God's Word appears in Christian curriculum. Word puzzles, mazes, jumbles, encoded messages, backward writing, hidden letters, rebuses, and r-bbits comprise the teaching method of choice.

The first stop in this part of our tour brings us to a major publisher's colorful page of jumbled and hidden words. We chuckled at this page's introduction:

God's Word isn't a jumble of words and thoughts. But here's a mixed-up game about God's Word that needs some straightening out.

We are to
L B A I N V S T E N O P R C

to God's Word

We are to be

D C A B C D O E R S F C H

not just listeners of the Word

Another curriculum features an encoded message for preteens. The message comes from Isaiah 43, but you need a telephone to solve it. Just follow the lettered keys on the phone to crack the code.

___ ___ ___ ___ ___ ___ ___, ___ ___ ___ ___ ___ ___ ___ ___
3   3   2   7   6   6   8   3   6   7   4   4   2   8   3

___ ___ ___ ___ ___ ___ ___ ___ ___ ___
7   3   3   3   3   6   3   3   9   6   8

If you can't figure it out, just grab that phone and dial 1-800-R-BBIT.

Here's another one from a different publisher that asks children to decode another message. Above each letter in the puzzle, kids are to write the letter that comes before that letter in the alphabet. The first couple of words have been done for you.

T o   d o ___ ___ ___ ___ ___ ___ ___ ___ ___ ___ ___ ___ ___
u p   e p   x i b u   j t   k v t u   u p

There's much more to this puzzle than we've shown here. It would take quite some time for Johnny to decode this one. We'd suggest he simply turn to Micah 6:8 and read the passage in plain language.

Now here's another favorite. Nearly all curriculum publishers fill student workbook space—and time— with word searches such as this one for junior highers:

There are 15 words from Genesis 1 hidden below. See how fast you can find them. They may be vertical, horizontal, diagonal, or backward. Then answer the question at the bottom.

```
M  N  P  O  E  H  X  U  Q  L  U
A  S  K  Y  T  G  B  H  U  J  D
C  C  T  R  W  O  A  F  V  S  O
E  R  A  R  V  D  T  M  W  U  O
G  E  B  E  G  I  N  N  I  N  G
I  A  Q  X  U  J  P  N  T  W  Q
S  T  A  R  S  D  A  Q  H  A  F
J  E  F  E  L  M  N  S  G  T  X
S  D  R  I  B  M  I  A  I  E  W
O  Z  P  X  G  F  H  U  L  R  B
```

In one sentence, what is the major truth of this passage?

Now, *we'd* like to ask in one sentence, why put young people through such tedious trivia?

Here's another one designed for teenagers.

Connect the dots in such a way that you spell out a riddle. The line you draw will visually provide the riddle's answer. Remember, the line will never cross itself. To get you started on the right track, the first part of the puzzle has been connected for you.

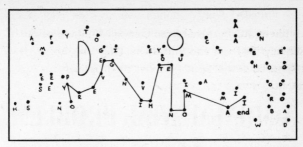

Next is another exercise for teenagers. They're asked to copy each group of letters and punctuation marks into the adjacent blanks. Then, when they've finished all that, they read vertically down each column to discover the words of Acts 1:1-2.

IHASEEVNGOD   _ _ _ _ _ _ _ _ _ _
NEBBAWESHTC   _ _ _ _ _ _ _ _ _ _
MOOECANTTHH _ _ _ _ _ _ _ _ _ _
YPUGHS,RHEO   _ _ _ _ _ _ _ _ _ _
FHTAUTAUEAS   _ _ _ _ _ _ _ _ _ _
OIANNAFCHPE   _ _ _ _ _ _ _ _ _ _
RLLTTKTTOON   _ _ _ _ _ _ _ _ _ _
MULOIEEILSA   _ _ _ _ _ _ _ _ _ _
ESTDLNROYTC   _ _ _ _ _ _ _ _ _ _
R,HOTUGNSLT   _ _ _ _ _ _ _ _ _ _
BIAAHPISPES   _ _ _ _ _ _ _ _ _ _
OWTNETVTIS1   _ _ _ _ _ _ _ _ _ _
ORJDDOIHRH: _ _ _ _ _ _ _ _ _ _
KOETAHNRIE1   _ _ _ _ _ _ _ _ _ _
,TSOYEGOTH-   _ _ _ _ _ _ _ _ _ _
TEUTHAIUTA2   _ _ _ _ _ _ _ _ _ _

Would that exercise make the teenagers you know really look forward to returning to church next Sunday?

Virtually every denomination sees an attendance drop-off among kids when they reach high school. After they've been subjected to teaching such as this, do you have any doubts as to why they might leave?

A MONUMENTAL PROBLEM

Remember, what you've seen here are not isolated examples. This type of busywork consumes 50 to 80 percent of most publishers' student materials. This is what occupies our kids' time week in and week out. This is the ghetto of Christian education.

Now, you may say some kids *like* puzzles and word scrambles. So does that justify the time they consume in church? Some kids like to crack their knuckles, too. So should we insert knuckle-cracking into all our curriculum? No, doing what a few kids like is not the goal of Christian education.

All these puzzles, fill-in-the-blanks, mazes, jumbles, crosswords, encoded Scriptures, and closed-ended questions produce virtually nothing. No one learns anything of substance—except that church and God and the Bible are aimless, tedious, confusing, boring, and a monumental waste of time. That's the hidden curriculum our students actually retain.

No wonder kids say Sunday school is "too much like school." Their young minds perceive that their Monday-through-Friday classrooms are also infused with irrelevance. Ohio author and education professor George Wood says, "Much of what students produce in school is artificial. That is, it has no purpose, no audience, no reason for existence beyond satisfying a teacher. Most kids get good at these exercises, figuring out that filling in blanks with words or phrases copied from the text is all they need to do."[2]

It's the public school model that the church has chosen to emulate. If a Christian curriculum doesn't look like what old-fashioned secular schools pump out, many assume it's not really curriculum at all. Truth is, the church has been duped.

NEW APPROACHES TO CURRICULUM

Some new, effective directions in curriculum are emerging—in the secular arena as well as Christian education. They exemplify much of what we've discussed in this book. They 1) remember the goal, 2) stress learning over teaching, 3) zero in on what's most important, 4) emphasize understanding, 5) promote thinking, 6) use active learning, and 7) use interactive learning.

We'll explore some interesting models that are achieving success in secular schools. And we'll share with you some of the work that we've been doing in Christian curriculum development. Our work grows out of our own experience, observations in the field, and interactions with hundreds of teachers, pastors, youth workers, religious education directors, and Sunday school superintendents. The curricular directions we've taken look nothing like the past.

We believe you'll find here some real hope, some practical approaches you can implement right away, and a peek at the future of education.

BEYOND TEXTBOOKS

For decades, schools and churches have relied on student textbooks and r-bbit-filled workbooks. These curriculum materials seemed so packed with information. Teachers assumed—hoped—that all the data contained in the books would somehow transmit to their students' brains. So these dry books became the focal point of the curriculum.

Now, education reformers are rethinking this single-minded reliance on student books. An innovative school in Minneapolis has found that today's kids are likely to learn far more, faster, with other methods. Mike Erdman, a third- and fourth-grade math teacher at the Tesseract school, doesn't start his students on fractions with a lifeless textbook. Instead, he begins with "manipulatives"—blocks and other objects—so kids can feel and see the difference between a third and a half.[3]

In Winnetka, Illinois, teachers and school officials have learned that kids learn little from traditional workbooks. So they've eliminated them completely. Classrooms here involve hands-on experience. Students see, touch, and smell what they need to learn. Their classrooms are filled with interesting stuff to help kids learn—gadgets and gizmos and costumes. And students help other students learn. Older kids tutor younger ones.

And in Mesa, Arizona, school administrator Susan Sprague and her colleagues have banned textbooks in the district's elementary science classes. They've found something better. They recognized that students forget almost everything they read or hear, but remember almost everything they experience directly.

These educators remember their goal. They want kids to understand relevant scientific principles—and gain a love for science. Both goals have been met in Mesa for almost 20 years now. Students know their stuff—and they actually go out of their way to learn more science. Sprague did a comparison test. She logged how many kids signed up for elective science classes when they entered high school. Of those kids who grew up with traditional, old-fashioned science classes, only four percent elected to continue with science. But of those who experienced Mesa's innovative, hands-on science classes, 96 percent chose more science classes! (Wouldn't it be wonderful if the church could instill that love for learning? Keep reading.)

"What's Mesa's secret?" you ask. Well, we wondered, too. So we traveled to this Phoenix suburb to see firsthand. What we found explained why educators regard this as the best district-wide science program in America.

If the textbooks are gone, what's in their place? Learning kits! Sprague and her resource specialists have developed over 100 different classroom science kits. The kits contain colorful objects that kids find fascinating. To understand buoyancy, third-graders work with clay to design boats that will float. To understand electrical circuits, high school kids try to make Christmas tree lights blink.

The district hires full-time clerks to fill these learning kits with their necessary ingredients and to keep them circulating among classrooms throughout the community.

We visited a fifth-grade classroom to see this kit-based learning approach in action. Student desks were bunched together in interactive-learning groups. Kids were buzzing around the room conducting research. The teacher moved from team to team, acting more like a coach and encourager than a disciplinarian.

The noise level was a bit higher than a traditional classroom. But the kids—all of them—were fully engaged. When the bell rang for lunch, nobody wanted to leave. The teacher had to chase them out!

This was a place of authentic learning.

Kids don't need artificial word jumbles and fill-in-the-blanks. But immerse them in activities they naturally take to, and they'll learn.

This concept drives the remarkable Key School in inner-city Indianapolis. Kids excel here, not through rote learning, but through a colorful array of intriguing experiences they help create. Principal Patricia Bolanos says, "Most schools are predicated on rewarding students for doing the things they ought to do. We've turned that around completely. We are saying that instead of coercing kids to do things, you give them chances to be involved in activities they relish."[4]

A REVOLUTION IN CHRISTIAN CURRICULUM

Many, many people complain about the state of education. Few do much about it. And that's been a large part of the problem. Plenty of critics and too few active reformers.

But the schools we've profiled above have moved beyond griping. They've created solutions that are producing impressive results. Can the church also respond to the challenge and consider some approaches to curriculum that will produce some life-changing results?

Well, we must admit that we, too, have spent the past couple of decades complaining about the state of education, particularly in the church. We kept hoping things would change. But we grew weary of waiting while new generations followed their predecessors—looking for the church's exit signs.

So we moved from the sidelines and began tinkering

with some revolutionary Christian curriculum ideas. One outgrowth of this process is Hands-On Bible Curriculum™ published by Group. At the risk of appearing self-promoting, we'd like to describe this new approach to children's curriculum. This case study shows that it's possible to incorporate the learning approaches prescribed in earlier chapters. Perhaps you'll find here a dose of hope and some ideas for curricular reform. And you'll get a peek at what curriculum for all ages will look like in the next century.

Hands-On Bible Curriculum consists of a teachers guide and a box of gizmos—called the Learning Lab™. There are no student books (kids told us they hated Sunday school workbooks). Everything the class needs is in the guide and the box. Each quarterly Learning Lab is filled with all sorts of colorful doodads that kids find captivating—prismatic eyeglasses, gooey stuff, disappearing ink, and holograms. There's also an audio cassette with interactive dramatic stories, unusual sounds, and sing-along music.

Each lesson features active learning and debriefing. Kids are never asked to sit and work crossword puzzles. Instead they experience—see, hear, touch, taste, and smell—their lessons, using the stuff in the Learning Lab.

At first glance, this Learning Lab and its colorful contents look "too fun" to some teachers. "Aren't these merely gimmicks?" they ask.

Just as Jesus fascinated the people he taught, the gizmos in Hands-On Bible Curriculum intrigue students and cause them to remember their lessons. "But won't they remember just the gizmo and not the biblical point?" doubters ask. Well, Jesus faced that risk, too. But he didn't stop teaching with captivating stuff.

After involving people in active-learning experiences, Jesus took the time to debrief his learners, so they'd get the real message. Debriefing is key. After picking grain on the Sabbath, he debriefed: "Have you not read what David did when he and the people with him were hungry?" (Matthew 12:1-8). After teaching about taxes with a coin, Jesus debriefed: "Whose image and name are on the coin?" (Matthew 22:15-22). After experiencing the sinful woman's teardrop-and-perfume footwashing, Jesus debriefed with a parable and a question (Luke 7:36-50).

Did all those people remember only the grain, the coin, and the perfume? Not likely. The message, cemented through debriefing, transcended the gizmos.

And, more than likely, the next time Jesus' learners saw one of his teaching objects in a different context, they thought of the lesson Jesus taught. The same will happen when we use today's objects to teach. Rather than fretting over the possibility that our learners will remember only the object, let us celebrate the fact that our students will think of their spiritual lesson whenever they encounter that object again.

One Hands-On lesson uses disappearing ink. But the kids don't realize this dark fluid is harmless when the teacher spills it on their clothing. They fret and begin to warn the teacher that their parents won't be happy when they come home with soiled clothes. The teacher says, "I'm so sorry. Will you forgive me?" Soon the ink blots disappear. And the teacher launches into a debriefing discussion on forgiveness. The kids recall their reactions when the teacher asked for their forgiveness. They grapple with the issues of everyday forgiveness. Matthew 6:12-15 is their scriptural guide. It's a memorable time.

"LESS IS MORE" CURRICULUM

This curriculum also breaks new ground in its emphasis on essentials. The disappearing-ink lesson, like all the lessons in this curriculum, has one simple point: God wants us to forgive others as he's forgiven us. That's it. During that one-hour session, the point is driven home time after time through a variety of multisensory experiences. Every student leaves knowing and understanding that one simple point.

All learning styles are utilized to emphasize the lesson's point. No matter if a child is a visual, auditory, or kinesthetic learner, he or she will get the point.

And this lesson does not try the glutton approach to Scripture. Just two passages from Matthew are used during the hour. But these forgiveness passages are injected in a powerful way. The objective is not to drown kids in Scripture, but to nourish them with what they can digest in a one-hour period.

> **"Genuine curricular reform needs to begin by acknowledging that not all of the facts we teach children will stick with them. But a habit of mind, something much more important, will stay with young people. It means covering less material, in more detail, and with more care."**

—*George Wood, Schools That Work* [5]

INTERACTIVE CURRICULUM

Another important feature of this new curriculum is that kids work together. They help each other learn. They support one another. They pray for one another.

Later in the forgiveness lesson, kids form pairs and tell each other about a time when it was really hard for them to forgive someone. This requires a bit of vulnerability that would never work as well in a large group setting.

The students grow accustomed to working in pairs and small groups. They form new friendships and anticipate returning the next week to be with their friends. In fact, one church reported that since switching to this curriculum, previously unchurched kids have been staying overnight on Saturday with their church friends—just so they can get to Sunday school the next morning!

Many, many churches have reported significant leaps in attendance since using this new curriculum. Teachers ask their students to recall their learnings—and the kids remember the lesson points from months ago. Parents report positive changes in their kids' behavior as a result of what they learned in Sunday school. And teachers who were at first wary of this unusual-looking curriculum find themselves caught up in its lively approach to learning. It makes teaching fun and rewarding.

This innovation in curriculum shows that it's possible to captivate today's kids, make them think, and help them discover God's life-changing truths.

MEANINGFUL INVOLVEMENT

Innovators in public education have also been pioneering some other approaches to curriculum. Ted Sizer, an education professor at Brown University, leads the Coalition of Essential Schools. This group of highly regarded schools runs on the principle that kids must show what they've learned, not on multiple-choice tests, but with exhibitions.

Here, from Sizer's book *Horace's School,* is an example of a student exhibition assignment:

Act as the school's nutritionist: the cafeteria has $2.56 to spend per full single serving for lunch. Design three menus, each of which is (1) within budget allowance, (2) maximally nutritious, and (3) maximally attractive to students in your school. You will have to consult the various tables and data displayed in the current nutritionists guide available in the library and the cafeteria office. Be prepared to defend your definitions of "nutritious" and "attractive" and your particular menus. You will submit your entries to an all-school poll, and the winning six menus will be served during the next term.[6]

At Kiva Elementary School in Scottsdale, Arizona, students learned about ancient Egypt by publishing a four-page newspaper called *King Tut's Chronicle.* It had a *National Enquirer* flavor with headlines such as "Cleo in Trouble Once Again?" The kids included a sports section (Nile boat races), an advice column ("Dear Cleopatra"), and financial news (price quotes on cloth for wrapping mummies). They learned history—and picked up skills in research, writing, and cooperation.

High school English students in Clayton, Georgia, research, write, edit, and publish Foxfire magazine. It's a collection of interviews with Appalachian elders and pieces on cooking, winemaking, and other country crafts. The magazine's contents have been compiled into the popular Foxfire books, sold nationally. The students learn grammar by doing. They take great pride in their work. And they never ask the question often heard in traditional schools: "Why do we have to know this?"

These examples illustrate the "direct purposeful experience" we discussed in chapter 6. Engaging students in meaningful projects such as these results in maximum understanding and retention.

RESUSCITATING CONFIRMATION

How can we translate this concept of meaningful involvement into church education? There are many opportunities. Let's look at an example that was applied to the educational process some churches call confirmation.

We consulted with a church on its confirmation program. These church leaders saw the statistics that show the negative hidden curriculum in many confirmation programs. Once young people are confirmed, most of them drop out of church. They "graduate," and they want out. Their confirmation education has the opposite effect of what their pastor intends. Confirmation confirms that church is dry, boring, tedious, and irrelevant. Many churches would accomplish more by offering nothing at all rather than the damaging confirmation programs they now offer.

In our consulting work, we helped the church know its goal for confirmation. The pastor and church leaders agreed the ultimate goal was to "encourage an abiding faith in Jesus Christ." With that goal as the target, we suggested that the existing confirmation curriculum be replaced with meaningful involvement projects like those described earlier.

One of these projects dealt with the theological concept of grace. We knew the old curriculum did not succeed in teaching this key tenet. So we suggested the junior-high-age confirmation class produce a *Candid Camera*-style show. The kids obtained a camcorder and found a hiding place in a local mall. While a couple kids operated the camera, the others stopped passersby and offered them money. They handed out free quarters! The shoppers were most bewildered. Some became quite angry. Most would not accept the coins! Everyone's reactions were recorded by the hidden camera.

After this afternoon of amusing entertainment, the kids returned to the church and watched their production. They howled as they watched their peers interact with the puzzled mall shoppers.

When the show was over, the pastor began the debriefing. "What did you think about how the people reacted to your free gift?" he asked. "Why do you suppose some people wouldn't accept this free gift? What were they afraid of? How was your offer of a free gift like God's offer of salvation? How were the mall people's reactions like how some people respond to God? What does God's free gift—we call it grace—mean to you?"

The kids talked about their *Candid Camera* project

for months. They organized a showing for their parents. These kids will likely remember the grace lesson for life.

A FAITH HISTORY PROJECT

The possibilities are endless for meaningful involvement projects. Some churches involve their young people in intergenerational faith history projects. Kids take cassette recorders and interview their parents and grandparents about their faith roots. They ask questions such as "When do you first remember praying to God? How did God become real to you? Describe a time when you doubted God. How did you overcome that doubt? When have you felt God's presence the most?"

This type of activity has powerful faith-growing possibilities.

The Search Institute study on Christian education found that a young person's conversations about God with his or her parents are the strongest single influence on that person's faith.

All too often parents don't know how to initiate faith talk with their kids. A project like this gives kids and parents a wonderful opportunity to talk about the most important subject in the world.

START CURRICULAR REFORM YOUNG

The curriculum you use makes a critical difference. This is true for all age levels. It's time for a revolution from preschool through adult classes.

We often hear church educators and pastors recognize the need for change in isolated age groups such as junior high or high school. But the problem of passive curriculum begins in the preschool department.

Many churches grow concerned when they see attendance and student interest begin to wane in fifth or sixth grade. When asked about the younger grades, educators often say, "No problem." They perceive no problem only because of the age of the customer—not because of the quality of the product. Teachers can more easily control smaller humans. And younger kids are less able to articulate their dissatisfaction. They're equipped with fewer persuasive skills to convince their parents they'd rather be elsewhere. But regardless of their immaturity, they are still victims of a curricular system that underestimates their abilities and chews up their precious time with mindless busywork.

Young children spend countless hours applying stickers to Sunday school papers. Their teachers were up till midnight the night before punching out those stickers. Young children's hands don't yet have the necessary motor skills to punch out their own stickers. So instead of preparing classroom activities that result in meaningful learning, teachers spend their preparation time toiling over stickers and looking for cotton balls and Popsicle sticks for the latest throwaway craft project.

All of that effort for minimal learning.

We must begin curricular reform with young children for another reason. The effective learning approaches discussed in this book, such as active learning and interactive learning, are far more successful with students after they've been exposed to these styles in their younger years. The reason today's teenagers struggle with thinking and problem solving is they've had few opportunities to flex their minds in earlier grades.

If we care about the spiritual growth of tomorrow's adolescents and adults we need to make big changes now in how we're teaching today's young children.

Let's remember the goal. We must not waste precious time subjecting our people to r-bbits and nonthinking busywork. If we care about kids and adults growing closer to God we must choose curricula that work.

The "DO IT" section that follows offers practical programming ideas to help you share and apply these principles in your church.

To incorporate curriculum that really works, review some of the sample activities in chapters 6 and 7. Next you'll see a combined-age lesson on prayer to give you an idea of what can be done with curriculum. Then you'll get a batch of idea catalysts for activities that bring depth to learning. They're not simulated activities; they're direct and purposeful, with meaning in and of themselves. At the chapter's conclusion you'll find a rating chart for analyzing your present curriculum.

IDEAS FOR COMBINED AGES

See how a teacher can use the following activity to engage learners of any age in the concept of prayer. This could even work with elementary-age children through adults learning together!

HOW GOD TALKS TO US

Ask for a volunteer to leave the room. Choose an older student who will reliably follow your directions. When the volunteer has left, show the rest of the class where you're going to hide honey and graham crackers.

Say: **When** (name) **comes back into the room, you're going to try to guide** (him or her) **to the honey and graham crackers by giving** the clues "hot" and "cold." No fair moving or pointing or giving any other clues. If (name) finds the honey and graham crackers within 30 seconds, everyone gets to share them.

Slip into the hall with the volunteer. Quickly explain he or she is just to stroll around the classroom and completely ignore the clues the other kids are giving.

Bring the volunteer back into the classroom.

Say: **Is everybody ready? The 30 seconds start . . . now!**

Notify kids when you're down to 20 and 15 seconds. Then, as their excitement mounts, count down the seconds from 10 to zero. Have everyone, including your volunteer, sit down. Warn kids that the location of the honey and graham crackers must still be kept a secret.

Ask:

● **How did you feel as** (name) **ignored your clues? Explain.** (Frustrated; I felt like I had to yell louder.)

● **What's so bad about** (name) **not paying attention to what you were saying?** (Now we don't get the honey and graham crackers; it seemed like a waste of time.)

● **How is** (name) **ignoring your directions like people who live their lives without paying any attention to what God has to say to them?** (They miss out on good things, too; they wander around and never accomplish much of anything.)

Say: **Okay, let's play this game again. This time** (name)**, pay attention to the clues everyone is giving you.**

Let the students call out "hot" and "cold" again to lead the volunteer to the honey and graham crackers. Have everyone give the volunteer a big round of applause. Then gather the class members in a circle, place the honey and graham crackers in the center, and ask:

● **How did you feel as** (name) **got closer and closer to the honey and graham crackers?** (Happy; excited.)

● **How is that like being tuned in to what God has to say to you?** (It's exciting; good things happen to us.)

● **What are some ways we can tune in to God?** (Reading the Bible; praying.)

Say: **We're going to eat the honey and graham crackers in just a minute, but first, let's look at what the Bible says.**

TUNING IN TO GOD

Have students turn to Psalm 119:97-104 in their Bibles. Have older kids read the psalm aloud, each reading one verse.

After the reading, bring out plastic knives and paper plates. (If possible, obtain a honeycomb and let kids examine it at this time. Some kids may be able to explain how and why the bees construct the honeycomb.)

Have each person dip a knife into the honey and spread the honey onto a graham cracker.

As people are enjoying their snacks, say: **Oh, no! I forgot! Would anyone rather have this for a treat?** Pull out a big white onion.

Kids will probably laugh as they assure you they'd rather have the honey and graham crackers.

Ask:

● **What's so good about honey?** (It's sweet; it's good for you.)

● **How is learning what the Bible says like eating honey?** (It's good and good for us; we don't want to stop.)

● **Why did the psalm writer compare reading the Bible to eating honey? Why didn't he compare it to eating an onion?** (Honey is a delicious treat; it's sweet and good, like God's Word; onions are hot and give you bad breath.)

● **What good things do you get from honey?** (Energy; vitamins.)

● **What good things do you get from reading the Bible?** (I learn about God's love; I get guidance for my life; I get comfort when I'm feeling sad.)

Say: **God talks to us through his Word. The Bible is like a personal letter written to each one of us. You know how fun it is to get letters in the mail—imagine getting a letter from God! You'd want to read it every day, over and over again. And I hope you will.**[7]

INVOLVEMENT PROJECTS

Plug in these project ideas to your church's curriculum. Use these ideas for memorable, meaningful lessons that students won't forget.

1. Campaign for it. Foster ownership in

what's studied. Form teams to work together to "campaign" for the book of the Bible they want to study. Have teams create banners, slogans, buttons, campaign speeches—the whole bit! After a spirited campaign "convention," have teams vote for which book of the Bible to study.

One junior high class campaigned, and Proverbs won the vote. Next they sponsored a cake sale at church to (get this!) buy personal Bible commentaries on Proverbs. Each cake sold came with a card telling about the kids' hope to buy commentaries for their Bible study group. People got excited about supporting the kids and were happy to buy a cake for the cause. The kids sold out and had enough money to buy all their commentaries!

The last we heard, the group was finishing scripting, directing, and producing a video on the book of Proverbs!

2. Post office. Build a large, official-looking mailbox for use as a three-dimensional bulletin board. Place it in a central spot. Announce times for mail pickups for people within the church.

Ask students to write words of kindness and encouragement to others in the church—not only friends, but also people they think could use a friend. After writing the notes, have students post them on the mailbox. Invite students to write thank you notes to people who've helped them— the pastor, teachers, ushers, readers, musicians, or custodian, for example. Encourage people to answer their letters. Watch relationships form and grow because of the new communication system.

3. Adopt a family. Find a needy family in your community. Have one class learn what the family needs most in terms of resources—clothing, food, baby-sitting, car repair, house cleaning. Have the class find ways to get food and clothes for the family; they can write letters or make cards; they can offer their services to the family; they can visit them. Reaching out in this way can make a lasting impact on class members.

4. Adopt a grandparent. Children, youth, or adults can reach out in a special way to the elderly and shut-ins. Class members can share hobbies, read, comb and style hair, run errands, write and read letters, and simply spend time listening. One young person grew very attached to her surrogate grandparent. She remembered how raisins were the woman's favorite treat and made sure she delivered some on special occasions. In an era when extended families live far apart, gaining wisdom from the elderly helps any age student.

5. Create a scrapbook. Have class members research different topics and choose one to explore in depth. For example, they could choose their own faith journeys, their denomination's history, Jesus' life, a book of the Bible, or a biblical character. Have teams spend time finding information and compiling it in a scrapbook to describe to the rest of the class and display for the congregation.

6. Make a movie. Today's easy access to video equipment makes it possible to bring Bible stories and church history to life. Let students research, script, star, direct, and produce their own show. Share it with the entire congregation. Depending on how elaborate you want to get, you could sell tickets and popcorn and make the premiere showing a big event!

7. Write a book. Assign classes to write and illustrate portions of a book. How about a seasonal devotion book for the congregation and community? The weeks leading up to Easter and Christmas make for special devotional times. Have the books printed and given away or sold. Families will treasure these important projects. Besides, they're a terrific way for people to express their faith in words and art.

8. Conduct interviews. Send class members on a mission to collect faith stories from people of all ages. Have students write their own interview questions, such as "Why do you believe in God? When has Jesus meant the most to you? How has the church met or not met your needs?" Have students compile them and share what the experience was like.

9. Involve families. Instead of splitting up family members during Sunday school time, get kids and parents together to talk about their faith and hot issues. Do lots of small group work in which you intersperse youth-to-youth, parent-to-parent, and youth-to-parent discussions. Some people fear uncomfortable situations if some kids' parents aren't there. Those children still need positive family and adult role models—even if they're not their own parents.

10. Brainstorm potential projects. The

HOW DOES YOUR CURRICULUM RATE?

Use these questions to analyze the strengths and weaknesses of your present curriculum. Take stock of the teaching methods used. If your curriculum needs improvement, ask what you can do to adapt or replace it.

1. What seems to be the overall goal of this material?

___ learn historical facts
___ emphasize understanding of relevant life principles

___ learn Bible vocabulary
___ clearly apply Scripture to students' daily lives

2. What are the tacit objectives?

___ teaching
___ learning
___ cover a lot of material
___ thorough understanding and retention
___ keep students busy
___ help students think
___ quiet, orderly classroom
___ active, learning students

3. Which is most encouraged: lower- or higher-order thinking?

___ fill-in-the-blank exercises
___ discovery learning
___ word games/ puzzles
___ thought-provoking activities
___ rote memorization
___ conceptual understanding
___ closed-ended fact questions
___ open-ended thinking questions

4. How is the Bible approached?

___ quotations to be memorized
___ practical truths to be understood

preceding list can be a catalyst for your church's classes. But projects can be even more meaningful when they're born out of specific needs unique to your group, church, or community.

___ stories from history   ___ guidance for students' daily lives

___ glutton approach—the more Bible per lesson the better   ___ digestible approach—each lesson provides a nourishing morsel

___ emphasis on biblical detail   ___ emphasis on essential teachings

5. Is the methodology more passive or active?

___ passive   ___ active

___ emphasis on receiving information   ___ emphasis on discovering truth

___ sitting still   ___ moving about

___ one or two senses involved   ___ several senses involved

___ teachers lecture   ___ students have conversations

___ students are the audience   ___ students learn by doing

___ boring, tedious   ___ fun and/or captivating

___ teachers tell   ___ teachers ask

6. What are the structures of learning?

___ individual or competitive   ___ interactive—students work in pairs and small groups

___ students rely largely on the teacher   ___ students often rely on each other

___ teachers do all the teaching   ___ students often teach each other

___ teacher-based   ___ student-based

Responses on the left side of this form indicate less effective learning approaches. Responses on the right side indicate curricular approaches that result in more genuine learning.

9 RENOVATE THE SERMON

When speaking of church education we rarely mention the sermon. Is this a teaching time? More importantly, is it a learning time?

Every week this time slot of 20, 30, or more minutes is reserved for the pastor's dispensing of content. In the vast majority of churches, the sermon is presented in the traditional teaching mode—straight lecture. One person talking from behind a podium. What really happens during this time? How much is learned? What's the goal of a sermon? What difference does this sacred time slot make? Is there a better way?

We polled adult church-attenders to learn their perceptions of the sermon time. Here's some of what we discovered:

- Just 12 percent say they usually remember the message.
- Eighty-seven percent say their mind wanders during sermons.
- Thirty-five percent say the sermons they hear are too long.
- Eleven percent of women and 5 percent of men credit sermons as their primary source of knowledge about God.

Regardless of your interpretation of these data, the sermon is still perceived as a vital part of church life. Another bit of research we conducted revealed that preaching is the #1 consideration when families with children select a church.[1]

It's a paradox. Parishioners often cite the sermon as the pinnacle of the worship service, yet they retain very little from it. How could this be? What do the pew-sitters feel they're receiving from their time commitment in front of the pulpit?

Perhaps the answer lies in society's general perception of preaching. The common image is not a positive one. Witness some oft-heard comments: "Nobody likes to be *preached* at." "Then she gave me this *sermon* about always being late." "He ought to practice what he *preaches*." In the vernacular, we rarely use the terms "sermon," "sermonize," or "preach" in positive ways. Over the years, preaching has picked up a bad connotation.

If we understand this reputation, we can begin to unlock the paradox. People enter the church with the societal expectation that they'll be "preached at." Hence, a "good sermon" is anything that makes that 20 or 30 minutes pass with a minimum of discomfort. We've trained people to seek comfort.

John Hull, author of *What Prevents Christian Adults From Learning,* says, "It does not matter to the listeners that they are unable to repeat even the main theme of the sermon five minutes later; the important thing is the comforting emotion of familiarity and belonging which swept over them as they were listening."[2]

Must we be content with merely transforming the distasteful into the comfortable? Is that all there is? Can't this weekly opportunity result in more learning than we've come to accept?

THE PROBLEM WITH PREACHING

Are lackluster speaking skills to blame for lackluster learning from sermons? Well, we've worked with a lot of pastors. And all of them believed they were above-average, gifted speakers. Our poll of church members found general satisfaction with preachers' speaking skills. Seventy-four percent said their pastors are above-average speakers.

Though we've all heard sermons that could cure the worst case of insomnia, that's not the central problem. The problem is far more basic. The problem lies within the medium itself.

The medium—straight speaking to a crowd—results in very little retention, very little learning. According to the publication *Communication Briefings,* people forget 40 percent of a speaker's message within 20 minutes. They forget 60 percent after a half day. And after a week they lose 90 percent. These figures apply to gifted speakers as well as lackluster ones. No matter how articulate the speaker, almost

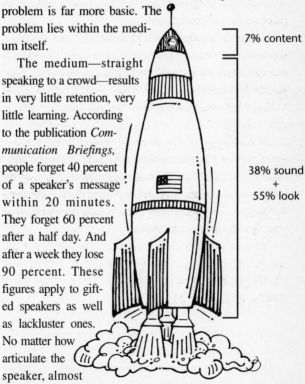

7% content

38% sound
+
55% look

everything he or she utters is quickly forgotten, forever lost and never applied by the vast majority of listeners.

Most preachers expend considerable effort researching and preparing the words of their sermons. They're often meticulous about their homiletics and theology. They usually grasp a thorough understanding of their material. But a thorough understanding of their medium eludes them.

Communication scholars understand the medium. A University of California study found that the words speakers so carefully choose actually carry a minimal part of the message. How the speaker sounds (inflection, tonality, voice variety, emphasis, and energy) communicates 38 percent of the message. And what the listeners see carries 55 percent of the message. This includes the speaker's appearance, gestures, movement, and visual aids. Only 7 percent of the message that listeners receive comes from the words themselves.[3]

Speaking experts sometimes depict spoken communication as a rocket. See the illustration on page 243. The sound and look of the message comprise the rocket's booster system. The words are the payload. Without a powerful and carefully prepared booster system, the payload will never arrive at its intended destination. A speaker's words—no matter how appropriate—have little chance of scoring without a strong launch.

A SHIRKING OF RESPONSIBILITY

Our ears are burning. Already we know what many readers—pastors—are muttering: "You Schultzes don't understand the nature of preaching the Word." We often hear a couple of arguments:

ARGUMENT #1: *"Preaching is a two-way street. The congregation has a responsibility to come to worship prepared—ready to listen."* This argument is often used to deflect complaints about anemic sermons. We heard a seminary president say, "If people come listening to see what they can get out of a sermon—asking, 'Does this apply to me?'—they probably won't get a lot out of the sermon."

This is a cop-out. It provides a handy excuse. If a bad sermon is half the listener's fault, the preacher feels only half bad—if at all. The quality of preaching will improve only when its practitioners accept full responsibility for their work.

The fact is, people *should* come to church asking, "Does this apply to me?" Their minds are all tuned to WIIFM—What's In It For Me? They're looking to be fed, to be challenged, to be assured of God's saving grace, to learn. That is their preparation. It's the preacher's job to cause learning to happen.

Former U.S. Secretary of Education Shirley Hufstedler said, "The secret to being a successful teacher is . . . to accept in a very personal way the responsibility for each student's success or failure. Those teachers who do take personal responsibility for their students' successes and failure . . . produce higher achieving students."[4]

ARGUMENT #2: *"I am nothing. The power of the Holy Spirit will work through even a poor speaker."* This argument defers to God the effectiveness of preaching.

It's true—the Holy Spirit can work through anything, anybody. Those who deliver God's Word do so with the assurance of built-in power. The Lord, in Isaiah 55:11, promises, "The same is true of the words I speak. They will not return to me empty. They make things happen that I want to happen, and they succeed in doing what I send them to do."

But it's also true that God trusts us to use the gifts and abilities that he's bestowed upon us. The Apostle Paul explained in his first letter to the Corinthians about the various giftedness of God's people. Those gifts include prophesying and teaching. Paul takes great care in cautioning his people about the perils of speaking in "different languages"—tongues. His words also have meaning for preaching today. "Unless you speak clearly with your tongue, no one can understand what you are saying. You will be talking into the air! It may be true that there are all kinds of sounds in the world, and none is without meaning. But unless I understand the meaning of what someone says to me, I will be a foreigner to him, and he will be a foreigner to me." (1 Corinthians 14:9-11).

Paul makes it clear we carry the responsibility to be effective speakers. No use blaming the Holy Spirit if the sermon winds up "talking into the air."

IF MADISON AVENUE PREACHED

Although the art of communication may not be well-understood by Sunday morning speakers, it is understood, well-researched, scrutinized, and perfected by those who specialize in it—advertising and marketing professionals. We thought it might be fascinating to ask Madison Avenue-types what they'd do with the sermon time. After all, both the preacher and the marketeer are in the persuasion business. Both attempt to affect the hearts and behavior of their audiences through the art of communication.

So we posed some questions to some professional persuaders in the advertising and marketing world. How would they approach a captive audience every week? If they had the incredible opportunity of addressing potential customers in a face-to-face encounter every week, what would they do? Would they try to persuade their customers by weekly sitting them in front of a lecturer who stands behind a big podium and simply talks at them?

The marketing professionals chuckled at our questions. Their answer to the last question: No—they wouldn't throw away a marvelous opportunity on a method that anyone in their profession knows has very little chance of success. Well, what *would* they do with this opportunity? Their answers centered around three solid maxims:

MADISON AVENUE'S PREACHING TIPS

1. KNOW YOUR PEOPLE.

Marketing people know they must first accurately assess their customers' nature, needs, and wants before attempting to persuade them. What are these customers feeling this week? How have certain events shaped their thinking this week? How are they changing? What's shaping their fears and hopes?

The marketing folks we consulted wondered how well most preachers handle basic needs assessment and market analysis within their congregations. Dallas advertising executive Debbie Benedek says, "As a sermon observer, I feel they don't know me at all."

In our sermon-listeners' poll, people told us preaching was most memorable when it touched on something they were experiencing in their day-to-day lives at that moment. No other preaching variable rated even close to the personal-life-relevance factor.

So, how can a pastor keep close to the pulse of the congregation? Won't all the personal interactions in committee meetings, potlucks, and counseling sessions supply the necessary market research? Too often this rather passive approach to knowing the audience fails to give an accurate or complete image of the Body's health. And the resultant sermons may miss the mark.

Proactive efforts can help sermons reach the Body's needs more effectively. One pastor utilizes a "sermon squad." This group of six or eight laypeople receives Scripture passages the pastor will be preaching on for the ensuing six months. Every Wednesday they complete and submit a brief questionnaire about the following Sunday's Scripture. The questions are quite simple: "What questions does this Scripture raise in your mind? What's happened to you lately that this Scripture speaks to? What changes need to take place in you and our members as a result of reading this Scripture?" These folks take their weekly responsibility seriously because they know the pastor uses their insights in his preaching. Every six months, a new set of members makes up the "sermon squad."

> **"I have become all things to all**
> **people so I could save some of**
> **them in any way possible."**
>
> —*1 Corinthians 9:22*

2. INVOLVE YOUR PEOPLE.

Do you know why so many of those offers you get in the mail include punch-out tokens, tear-off stamps, rub-off spots, and scratch-and-sniff fragrances? Because the advertising professionals know that once they involve you, you're much more likely to respond to their offer. It's a well-proven bit of human nature.

And the marketing pros we consulted said they'd find some way of involving congregation members during the sermon time.

Former New York marketing executive Tom Turner remembered a presentation he made for Doubleday cookbooks. Toward the end of the presentation, the doors swung open and a waiter and waitress entered pushing carts loaded with goodies baked from the cookbooks' recipes. Everyone in the audience got a taste. That was 20 years ago. And to this day, Turner still hears from people who remember that meeting.

The possibilities are endless for involving the congregation in the sermon. One pastor's Thanksgiving sermon included the distribution of thank you cards to everyone. The pastor asked each person to take a moment right then to fill out the card to someone for whom he or she was thankful. Then he asked his people to deliver their cards the next week. The stories he heard back from parishioners' experiences became wonderful future sermon illustrations. And the people never forgot that involving sermon.

Here's another simple way to frequently involve listeners during the sermon: Ask them to talk with a partner or small group of three or four. This interactive technique can be used in a variety of ways. It's an engaging sermon starter. For example, for a sermon on doubt ask parishioners to turn to a partner and tell about a time when their faith was shaken.

This method can also be used for honing understanding and retention. Warn listeners they'll soon be required to summarize or explain a concept from the sermon. They'll start listening more attentively. Then, at the right moment, say, "Okay, turn to a partner and explain this concept in your own words." Stephen Covey, author of *The Seven Habits of Highly Effective People,* uses this interactive technique extensively in his seminars. Everyone goes away learning a lot.

Another audience involvement device mentioned by our marketing consultants is quite obvious. It's as simple as asking, "Any questions?" Turner says, "As soon as you get a little bit of give and take, you're there. You've got them because you can zero in on the things that are most important to them."

Rev. Lee Hovel in Mission, Kansas, allows time for questions at the end of his sermons. He finds that people learn more because of the opportunity to interact with the preacher. Parishioners can clear up confusion, get more information, and even disagree with the sermon. As we discussed in chapter 5, when we encourage our people to ask faith questions, they tend to think, and their faith tends to grow.

The questions also help Hovel know his people. "I know when there are no questions from the sermon, somehow I didn't touch something in their life," he says.

This technique requires a degree of vulnerability from the pastor. But that display of vulnerability creates spin-off benefits. "Being vulnerable yourself as the pastor," Hovel says, "creates an openness in other people to be vulnerable with you." Hovel's members report they feel more comfortable approaching him since he began the give-and-take sermons.

3. USE VISUALS.

The marketing people said they'd never attempt to persuade a crowd without using their most powerful tool—visuals. They know that most people (more than 80 percent) are visual learners.[5] In order to ensure that a message sticks, people need to see it.

Sermon visuals can include props, handouts, film clips, short dramatic presentations, and overhead transparencies with key words or drawings.

We recognized a lost opportunity at Joani's 94-year-old grandmother's funeral. The preacher described how this beautiful Christian woman died while serving others. She collapsed while making popcorn balls for neighborhood children. That was a perfect parting picture of this lifelong servant of God. The preacher could have galvanized that point in his listener's minds forever by the simple use of a visual. If only he'd brought out Grandma's last batch of popcorn balls at that moment!

No one present that day would have ever looked at a popcorn ball again without thinking of the Christian witness demonstrated by the little old woman who served others until her last breath.

Marketing and advertising people know how to persuade. And so did Jesus. He used the same techniques. He knew his people, he involved them in his messages, and he used visuals lavishly.

CHILDREN'S SERMONS

"People—adults—tell me they get more out of the children's sermon than the regular sermon."

How often have you heard that?

Let's stop and take that children's sermon quote seriously. (Those who say it are quite serious, we assure you.) What is it about children's sermons that often make them connect with people of all ages? Why can't any sermon use the qualities that make children's sermons shine? Good children's sermons...

● ...assume nothing. Children's pastors are less likely to use churchy jargon. They know they'll lose some kids if they do. Big words, if they're used at all, are explained so young minds can follow. Hard-to-grasp concepts—like the Trinity—are carefully illustrated to enlighten the uninitiated. Well, copious research tells us the adults in the pews need help with the basics, too.

● ...make one point. They don't fall into the quagmire described in chapter 3. "Less is more" in children's sermons. Seminary professors who still teach the three-point sermon do a great disservice. Listeners—of any age—cannot digest and retain everything a three-point sermon tries to cram into a limited attention span. It's the law of the farm. Planting too many seeds in a tiny plot will not yield a greater harvest. Children's sermons succeed because they typically make one simple point, over and over, in simple language. A preacher, standing before a congregation of any age, will cause more learning by making one point well—and then concluding.

● ...**appeal to the senses.** Somehow we know that little kids learn best when we involve more than one of their senses. So, children's sermons often include props to look at, sounds to hear, fuzzy objects to touch, sweets or salts to taste, and fragrances to smell. Engaging multiple senses does indeed greatly enhance learning—in people of any age.

● ...**allow time for give and take.** Children's pastors often ask questions of their listeners—and invite questions from them. This interactive format puts minds in gear. Audience participation makes learning blossom.

If sermons for grown-ups became a lot more like children's sermons, people of all ages would learn more.

STARTING OVER

Imagine with us for a moment. If you'd never attended even one church service, if you hadn't "always done it that way," would you try to persuade, inspire, or motivate a room full of people by merely talking at them from behind a podium?

You'd know better. You'd know you have many other more powerful tools at your fingertips to cause people to learn. You wouldn't squander such a wonderful opportunity on a medium that, by itself, has a relatively minimal impact.

Imagine this is a new day. You have license to start over. Shake up your congregation by taking a new approach to preaching that really makes a difference.

The "DO IT" section that follows offers practical programming ideas to help you share and apply these principles in your church.

Try these "memory-makers" to bring God's message alive during the sermon time. All of these have been tried and rank among listeners' unforgettables.

SERMON MEMORY-MAKERS

● **Turn to a partner**—Smack-dab in the middle of a sermon, have the pastor ask the listeners to turn to a partner, making sure everyone has someone to talk to. Have listeners tell, "The last time I saw God working in my life was..." For many people it can be a time to verbalize their faith to another congregation member, a family member, or a visitor. It's a great opportunity to practice "faith talk" in a nonthreatening environment.

The variations are many. Use pair-shares or small groups to help people grapple with a specific sermon point; have people tell one another what they'll do in their lives this week as a result of the sermon (this has the added benefit of building in accountability among members); encourage partners to share prayer concerns. Let people experience their fellow members of the body of Christ.

● **Be vulnerable**—Here's something that showed up on our surveys of unforgettable sermons. Listeners are moved by the preacher's ability to be real with them. This takes all forms, but probably the most poignant was this true story:

The sermon's topic was forgiveness. Earlier that morning, the pastor admitted he had yelled at his wife about not having matching socks available for him. In front of the congregation, he asked his wife for forgiveness. His vulnerability deeply touched the people and modeled a powerful, relevant example for them.

● **Reflection on how God meets your needs**—Before the sermon begins, have each person spend a few minutes in silence (a strange thing to do in this fast-paced world). As people quietly pause, they can reflect on what they need to hear from God. Is it a word of encouragement? confrontation? strength? courage? After a few minutes have them reflect on someone in their lives. What does that person need most from God that day? Because people spend time focusing on their needs, God seems to speak more clearly.

This reflection also works well following a sermon. Allow time and prayer for listeners to decide how their lives will be different because of the message heard.

● **Eavesdropping**—One memory-maker happened when the pastor sat in a recliner, facing away from the congregation. While carrying on a personal conversation with God, the casual approach helped listeners learn that they too can talk to God as a friend.

● **The people who sat in darkness**—Use John 1 as the sermon's framework. Preach the entire sermon in the dark. Keep everyone in darkness until the Light shines, as you tell of Jesus Christ. One by one let each person light their own votive candle. Allow the congregation to feel Jesus' power coming into their lives as they feel the warmth and witness the glow of light.

● **Priorities straight?**—One Sunday morning the pastor went to the pulpit and said, "I'm sorry. I've been so busy this week I didn't have time to prepare a sermon. It's just been one of those weeks." Then he sat back down.

The congregation was incredulous! What do you mean too busy? He just sat there long enough to make everyone very uncomfortable.

He finally returned to the pulpit. Only this time with another message. He spoke about priorities—that we've all been given 24 hours a day to spend as we choose. It's not that we're too busy to do things, it's that we don't choose to do some things. He etched his point by evoking strong emotions in people.

● **Take action**—To spur congregation members into action, hand out a specific "to do" list on the topic. For example, after one sermon, people were encouraged to write their congressional representatives, support a program with their money, and pray for that program.

Too often we leave it up to the listeners to figure out what they're supposed to do with the sermon information. It may not always be a specific program—but it may be a specific action, such as telling a significant person in your life you love him or her, reaching out in forgiveness to the person you're holding a grudge against, or counting to 10 when you feel like blowing up at the person who angers you.

● **Thanksgiving offerings**—Prior to a Thanksgiving service the people were asked to bring a symbol of what they were most thankful for that year. All ages could participate. As people came forward to place their symbols on the altar, the experience was very moving. One farmer hobbled forward with an ear of corn, a new grandmother brought a doll to represent her new grandchild, and a little boy brought a picture of his family.

● **Involve the listeners**—The transfiguration of Christ gave a new twist to a sermon about being strengthened to reach out. The pastor brought forward about 10 volunteers. He formed two circles, side by side to form a figure 8. One circle faced inward with everyone's arms outstretched toward the center. The other circle faced outward with arms outstretched. With everyone holding their arms straight out in front of them, the people began to

move in a figure 8. As they moved they created a visual message, as their arms faced inside the circle, then outside the circle. It illustrated the need to come together to rejuvenate with God's Word, and then have strength to reach out to others.

● **A lamp to share**—One pastor used an oil lamp in his sermon to show how we are all lights in the world. Only he didn't stop there. He said, "Sometime this week I'll give this lamp to someone in the congregation who's been a light for me the past year. After that person receives the lamp, he or she can pass it on to someone else in the congregation who's been a light to that person." What a wonderful way to spread the light!

ACTIVE CHILDREN'S SERMONS

Now you'll find some sample children's sermons. It's messages like these that stick with listeners and make an impact on learning.

TUG OF WAR

You'll need a 20- to 25-foot rope or clothesline.
Lay the rope in a long line on the floor. Read the text: "So what should we say about this? If God is with us, then no one can defeat us" (Romans 8:31).
Say: **If God is for us, who can be against us? Paul, who wrote the book of Romans, is talking about a war. It's like the game Tug of War.**

Let's play the game with boys against girls. Who do you think will win? *(Let children respond.)*

Okay, let's get several boys on one side and two girls on this side. *(Choose several boys and two of the smallest girls to play.)*

Hm. Something's not right here. There are only two girls versus all of these boys. We need some help. *(Look over the congregation and choose two of the biggest men to help the girls.)* (Names of the two men), **would you please come here and help the girls?**

(Have the two men join the girls on their side of the rope. The boys will probably complain that this is unfair.) **Why is this unfair? There are still only two girls!** *(The boys will tell you the men are bigger and stronger.)* **Oh, now I see! It's like what the verse in Romans says. No matter how many problems we have, if we have God on our side, we'll win. When you have people as strong as** (name the two men), **you stand a good chance of winning.**

Sometimes we feel there's too much ganging up on us. But God is on our side. And if God is for us, who can be against us?[6]

A PLACE FOR EVERYONE

Enlist the help of the choir. Have them prepare a simple four-part song for the message.

Have children gather in front of the choir. Say: **Each of us has different but special talents. And while your talent** (name a child sitting near you), **is not the same as your talent** (name another child), **that talent is just as important.**

As a matter of fact, when we use our talents together, we can make beautiful music.

That's the way the choir is. A choir is made up of four different parts. There's the bass section. These people sing really low. Let's hear the bass section. *(Basses sing a low note.)*

Then there are tenors. They sing a little higher than the basses. *(Tenors sing a note above the basses.)*

The people with low voices are called altos. *(Altos sing a note.)*

And finally, way up on top, are the sopranos. *(Sopranos sing a note.)*

Now what if the basses decide that only they should sing? Here's how it would sound. *(Basses sing the chosen song with only their part.)*

What if the altos insist on singing alone? *(Altos sing only their part of the song.)*

Since the sopranos usually sing the melody, they might think they're the most important and they should sing by themselves. *(Sopranos only sing.)*

That's what some people do, you know. We forget God gave us all different talents. We sometimes think only our talent is the one that counts. Or we may think someone else's talent is better than our talent.

No matter how big or small you are, God made you very special. And God wants you to use the gifts he gave you.

I think it's time for the choir members to use all their talents at the same time. Let's stand and direct the choir as they sing together.

(The choir sings the song.)

Wasn't that wonderful? Every choir member used his or her voice to praise God. That's what we can do, too. (Read 1 Corinthians 12:27: "All of you together are the body of Christ. Each one of you is a part of the body.")

No matter who you are or how different you are, God has a place for you. All you have to do is use the talent God gave you.[7]

10 WELCOME CHANGE

You now know why nobody learns much of anything at church. And you know how to fix it.

But that's not enough.

Knowing what's wrong and what's right is not enough. Knowledge without action serves little purpose. The church will never become a place of potent learning until its people are willing to change. And mustering the courage to change may present the biggest challenge of all.

Not long ago we conducted a nationwide survey about Sunday school curriculum among Christian educators. One of our questions to these folks was so obvious: "If you found a curriculum that you believed was superior, that would result in greater learning among your people, would you be inclined to switch from what you're using now?" Only 29 percent said yes.

What a shame. So many are willing to deny their students the opportunity to grow closer to God because of some other goal—to maintain the status quo, to cling to official but less effective sectarian materials, to refrain from rocking the traditional boat, to escape the fear of change itself.

But change we must. As Jesus illustrated in the parable of the talents, it's not enough to bury our treasure. God expects us to actively use the knowledge and gifts he's given us. God calls us to change, to grow, to lead others to change and grow.

In the church, that can sometimes seem akin to working miracles.

LIVING IN DENIAL

Resistance to change takes on many forms. Denial, in its various varieties, provides a convenient barrier to change.

When confronted with the problems of learning in the church, many folks simply deny any problems exist. "What's the big deal?" they ask. "Other churches may have problems. But we're doing just fine here the way we are."

Sadly, the church often follows a self-destructive path when it encounters conditions that call for substantial change. Christian researcher George Barna titled one of his popular books *The Frog in the Kettle*. He likens the church to a frog that's placed in a kettle of room-temperature water. Slowly the water temperature is turned up. The frog stays in the kettle, happy with its surroundings, unaware of the growing danger of its changing environment. Gradually, ever so gradually, the burner is turned up until the water boils—and the frog dies. The frog is content until the end, but nevertheless dead.

"Like the frog," Barna writes, "we are faced with the very real possibility of dying because of our unresponsiveness to the changing world around us."[1]

This contentedness has freeze-dried learning in the church. But we're not alone. America's public schools suffer because of denial, too. Even though American schools lag behind most of the industrialized world, most parents say their kids' schools are doing just fine. This kind of blind optimism causes deep problems to plague generation after generation.

Another form of denial can be characterized by the acronym MOTSH. It represents MORE OF THE SAME HARDER. Many who resist change recognize some problems. But they choose to handle the problems by intensifying the behaviors that caused their problems in the first place. "If only we do more of the same harder, maybe things will get better," they plead.

MOTSH thinking prevails in many schools. Officials often cite the need for reform, but resist any real change to address the problems. Instead they push the same tired old methods that created many of the problems initially. One Ohio teacher says, "The list of reforms was the most antistudent list we could imagine. More tests, more homework, more drill, more hours, more days. It's as if we are to just do more of what isn't working now."[2]

In the church we see the same MOTSH tendency. If kids don't know the Bible, religious educators order more of that old curriculum filled with Bible crossword puzzles. If the fourth-graders seem bored, teachers force them to sit still and listen to more teacher talk. If the congregation doesn't seem to respond to the sermon, the pastor preaches longer, louder. If the teenagers don't respond to the Bible study, youth leaders announce it's for "serious Bible students only." These MOTSH responses have severely crippled learning in the church.

> **"Churches that struggle often seek to maintain programs that are failing, believing that sufficient tinkering will breathe life into those programs."**
>
> —*George Barna, User Friendly Churches* [3]

One of the more curious forms of denial is practiced by the church's academic community. We recently watched a noted Christian education professor open a presentation by telling his audience that lecture-oriented teaching results in very little learning. Then, for the next 45 minutes he stood and lectured. He warned that people remember less than 10 percent of what they hear in lectures. He preached that Christian educators must actively involve their students. He *said* all the right things. But never once did he involve his listeners. His own teaching methodology betrayed his message.

It's astonishing how often we hear leaders in academia accurately target the deadly viruses of education, yet even in their diagnostic presentations they infect their audiences with the very approaches they condemn. Joani attended a national conference for experiential educators where all the presenters delivered straight lectures in front of passive audiences. Hour after hour they lectured one another about the ineffectiveness of the lecture method of teaching.

AN URGENT NEED FOR CHANGE

We're not advocating change for change's sake. We're advocating change for our people's sake. Their spiritual growth is at stake. The hidden curriculum in many churches is causing more harm than good. We simply cannot afford to maintain the status quo of learning in the church.

It's time to change—even though many don't recognize the need for change. We're facing an unhealthy but preventable predicament not unlike the medical findings of recent years. Before the medical community taught society about the dangers of certain behaviors, we all saw no need for change. Tobacco, fatty foods, and cholesterol were an unquestioned part of life for millions. No one saw the need for change.

Sitting down in front of a heaping plate of fatty, high cholesterol food was a happy habit for millions. "Why change? I like this food!" they cried. They were oblivious to the fact that they were gradually clogging their arteries and slicing years off their lives. They were suffering from a disease they didn't know they had, treading down a dangerous alley with no cognizance of what lurked in the darkness.

Similarly the church is slowly suffocating itself even though it's largely oblivious to its unhealthy habits.

We must sound the alarm. We must jolt the church into recognizing its self-destructive habits of education. The church doesn't realize it's infected with a life-draining disease.

Secular education is just now diagnosing its disease. Reformers are working to stem the epidemic that's plagued classrooms from kindergarten to graduate school. In late 1992 a committee of college and university presidents said teachers must abandon traditional methods such as lecturing students and requiring memorization of facts. Instead, they must show students how to get information and become independent thinkers, according to a report by the Presidents' Commission on Teacher Education of the American Association of State Colleges and Universities.[4]

The good doctors of education are calling for abandonment of dangerous habits. They're calling for fundamental change. Both our schools and our churches must change or be content with becoming sicker.

Researchers have found that change-resistant churches stagnate. But those who slay their sacred cows and embrace necessary change tend to grow. And, more important, their people grow—grow in faith.

According to a Search Institute study on Christian education, effective Christian education programming is what most encourages spiritual growth in a congregation. But the directors of this study recognized that Christian education's vast potential will never be realized unless the church is ready for major change in its approach to learning. In their research report, Peter Benson and Carolyn Eklin wrote:

> **"The need for change in Christian education parallels, in urgency and complexity, the need for change in public education. A recent review of public school reform efforts since 1985 suggests that schools have taken two different approaches to change. One approach is called 'tinkering,' in which schools attempt to increase effectiveness by adding one or two new program features without modifying the underlying educational assumptions, structure and format. The other approach is called 'restructuring,' in which schools introduce new models of teaching and learning. The report argues that the national effort to reform schools has largely failed because most schools have opted for tinkering."[5]**

We can't afford to stand still. And we can't afford to tinker. The time has come to change. Not tweaking change, but revolutionary change. We must restructure how people learn in the church.

UNDERSTANDING THE CHANGE PROCESS

To be successful in leading change, we must understand the process of change itself. People follow fairly predictable patterns when facing necessary change. Let's look at three stages of change that occur in all kinds of life situations. These apply to the lives of individuals, organizations, businesses, and churches.

STAGE 1: STATUS QUO

- Everything seems to be fine.
- The present modes of operation have been invented and have seemingly passed the test of time.
- Habits, systems, and bureaucracy grow.
- Rules and regulations are put into place.
- "Immune systems" attempt to stop anyone from changing the pattern.
- The focus shifts away from the original goal or actual constituents.
- Control becomes the goal.

STAGE 2: DANGER

- Conditions change.
- The old ways no longer fit the new circumstances.
- Effectiveness deteriorates.
- People begin to leave.
- Discomfort grows.

STAGE 3: DECISION

At this stage individuals and organizations choose between a couple of paths. One leads toward death while the other leads toward new life.

Path to Death	Path to New Life
● Fear of losing control.	● Acceptance of new circumstances.
● Confusion: "What's happening?"	● Examination of new options.
● Denial: "What problem?"	
● MOTSH: More of the same harder.	● Find a new pattern.
● Rationalization: "This will pass."	● Focus on potential gain from change.
● Anger: "It's your fault."	● Take a risk.
● Sense of loss.	● Choose to change.
● Death.	● Grow.

Some who choose the path to death simply smother. Others work through the process to the point of feeling a sense of loss, then gradually accept the necessary change. They eventually become a part of the new pattern but experience a lot more pain in the process.

Picture these three stages from an airplane pilot's perspective. See the illustration on page 271. In the first stage our plane and its passengers cruise along, oblivious to coming danger. In the second stage the plane encounters freezing rain. The airframe begins to take on a heavy, deadly load of ice. In the third stage our pilot must make a decision. Remaining too long in these conditions will lead toward death. Accepting the need for change and climbing to an ice-free altitude will lead toward safety and new life.

STAGES OF NECESSARY CHANGE

STAGE 1:
Status Quo

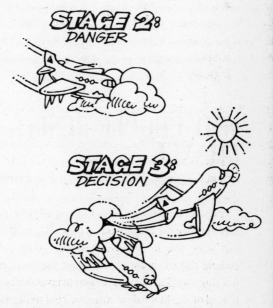

STAGE 2:
DANGER

STAGE 3:
DECISION

Different people handle change in different ways. A small number of people—about 5 percent—anticipate change. They see the value in a change before the need for that change actually arises. In our airplane illustration, the "anticipators" would climb to a high, safe altitude before ever encountering the freezing rain.

Another set of folks—the "early adopters"—tend to change during the first signs of danger. These people would climb to a safe altitude upon spotting the first evidence of ice accumulation on the airframe. About 10 percent of us are early adopters.

The third set of people make up the vast majority—about 85 percent. These are the "change resisters." They usually make changes—if any—when the surrounding pain or danger becomes too uncomfortable. These folks would wait until the plane picks up a dangerous load of ice before considering a change of altitude.

WHY PEOPLE RESIST CHANGE

Why would most people sit and watch their airplane ice up before taking corrective action? We've observed a number of reasons why people resist change.

1. They're *content*. They've grown accustomed to their ways. They bask in the familiarity of their environs. They're satisfied with the status quo—no matter how dangerous, outdated, or ineffective it may be. When it comes to learning in the church, they're satisfied with the present paltry results. When confronted with the fact that church members pick up only tiny bits of learning, they'd say, "Well, it's better than nothing."

2. They *lack understanding*. They don't understand either the problem or the suggested solution. If you'd point out that the church's educational efforts aren't working, they'd have trouble seeing how that could be possible. If you'd suggest changes, they'd be puzzled as to how those solutions would work.

3. They're *not willing to pay the price*. Even if they understand the need for a change, they resist supporting it because they don't believe it would be worth the time, effort, money, or trouble. They may see the reasons for changing the church's curriculum, but to them it wouldn't be worth the price of researching a new alternative, retraining teachers, or orienting students.

4. They're *tradition-bound*. Their motto: "That's the way we've always done it." The mere thought of change—any change—seems sacrilegious. Suggestions for changes in children's Sunday school would be met with "When I was a child we did it the old-fashioned way. If it was good enough for me, it's good enough for today's kids."

5. They *fear a loss*. When a new idea is proposed, their thoughts automatically go to what they'll lose if the new idea is implemented. "If we switch to that new curriculum," they'd say, "we'll have to throw out our old curriculum, our flannelgraph animals won't get used, our curriculum supplier won't like us anymore, the denominational office might find out, it'll cost more money, some teachers might get mad," and on and on.

"In times of rapid change, our experience becomes our worst enemy."

—*J. Paul Getty*

A GAME PLAN FOR CHANGE AGENTS

So, how do we overcome all these obstacles to change? How can we make learning work in an institution that has stifled learning for so long? Here are some practical tips.

1. Articulate the need. Many church folks are like the cholesterol and fat gluttons of the past. They're perfectly content with their old habits. They simply don't know they're self-destructing. But their ignorance won't save them from ultimately hurting themselves—and others.

People must first understand the problem. They won't be interested in changing their habits until they're convinced their habits are harmful.

Share with leaders, pastors, parents, and teachers some of the statistics cited in this book. Collect your own data about the learning gaps in your church. Show this book's companion video. It contains some compelling sequences that will inform your people of the need for change in your church's educational approaches.

2. Shift the focus to the gains of necessary change. When confronted with a potential change, most people begin thinking about what they'll lose. Change agents help them focus on what they'll gain.

We recently led a retreat for our own church's leadership team. We advocated identifying and pursuing a general vision for the congregation. We pointed out that strong churches are known for their vision, their sense of direction. Some churches specialize in community service while others focus on evangelism, small groups, music, contemporary worship, youth ministry, or Christian education.

Some of our leaders began to squirm. "If we begin to emphasize one area, we might offend members who aren't interested in that emphasis," they said.

We advocated change. Their minds automatically darted to the loss column. So we went to work redirecting their attention from what they'd lose to what they'd gain. We informed them that when churches adopt a good vision, the specialization attracts new members. And these new members possess other interests that enable the churches' other ministries to grow. If a church attracts people because of its excellent music, then its Bible studies, women's groups, and missions programs will grow, too. Much is gained.

When advocating changes in learning approaches you'll hear people fret about what they'll lose. Refocus their attention on what they'll gain:

- spiritual growth
- students who understand
- people whose thinking is challenged
- classes in which all students learn
- people who hunger for more of God's Word
- formation of new friendships
- people who remember what they've learned
- the inclusion of learning disabled students
- congregational and denominational loyalty
- reduced dropout rate
- consistent or increased attendance
- more effective outreach to the unchurched
- changed lives

Every time someone voices a feared loss, suggest another potential gain. Be prepared with a long list of gains for your church. Be persistent and reassuring in promoting these gains.

3. Understand that there is no such thing as a change that makes everyone happy. This is another tough concept for church folks who shudder at the thought of displeasing anyone—even temporarily.

Change—any change—will rile somebody. But should we shun change because of that? All human progress has been made with—and in spite of—voices of opposition.

They scoffed at Orville and Wilbur Wright.

Grover Cleveland said, "Sensible and responsible women do not want to vote."

The King of Prussia pooh-poohed railroads, saying, "No one will pay good money to get from Berlin to Potsdam in one hour when he can ride his horse in one day for free."

And our great teacher, Jesus Christ, was opposed at every turn because he advocated change. But he did not cease advocating change simply because change made some people uncomfortable. He knew that change would not come easily or smoothly.

That's probably one of the reasons he enlisted helpers—disciples—at the beginning of his change campaign. Surrounding himself with like-minded change agents helped make change more feasible. We can do the same.

Our cohorts help us influence others. And they help to buoy our own spirits when we run up against inevitable naysayers.

When we fixate on those who oppose change, we succumb to the same fear that cripples the opposers—the fear of a loss. Again, we must redirect our own thoughts to the gains the change will bring.

4. Don't try to implement all necessary changes at once. Guide your people through the process of change a step at a time.

Think back over some of the major elements of change we've discussed in this book:

- cover less material more thoroughly
- communicate what's most important
- pursue understanding
- ask good questions
- allow think time
- reduce reliance on memorization and lecture
- use active learning
- debrief all activities
- help learners teach one another interactively
- use a curriculum that works
- sculpt sermons that result in authentic learning

If you'd try to implement all these changes at once, you'd confuse and confound your people. Pick a couple of objectives and begin introducing them. Then add a couple more. And so on.

As you make innovations, support your people. Remind them of the vision. Reassure them that change, though perhaps uncomfortable at first, becomes more comfortable with time.

Our son eyed his new bicycle on his fifth birthday with some apprehension. He'd grown accustomed to his tricycle and couldn't see the real value of a two-wheeler. Eventually he pedaled his bike up and down the driveway with the help of his training wheels. He adapted to the change. Months later when we suggested removing the training wheels he howled in protest. But we assured him that Dad would run with him as he adapted to this latest change. Soon the boy was pedaling up and down the street with great confidence. He accepted the change a step at a time.

So, make big plans for revolutionary change. Create a big vision. Then implement it a step at a time. But don't stop. Keep progressing. Develop an environment of expectant change.

Begin by establishing your church's goal for learning. Evaluate your current programs and curricula. Change—choose more effective options. Train your teachers, leaders, pastors, and parents in the approaches that result in genuine learning.

THE FIRST STEP

The first step is to begin. No change will occur without action. Simply thinking about the problem won't make it go away. Action is required.

Knowledge isn't enough. Many people already know that learning in the church is failing. Now is the time to change, to begin a revolution of learning that can transform the church.

Start today. Tomorrow is too late.

The "DO IT" section that follows offers practical programming ideas to help you share and apply these principles in your church.

DO IT

Here you'll find tips for exploring change. They'll help you jump-start people's thoughts about change and what that could mean for learning in your church. Use these ideas with teachers, parents, adults, and other people who could help make change happen. How about church committee members? all your church teachers? a small group of change agents who've volunteered to explore learning in your church? Choose one or more of the following activities to actively engage these people in the change process.

ACTIVITIES FOR LEARNING CHANGE

HANDWRITING ANALYSIS

Ask people to sign their names the way they usually do. Then have them each place their pen or pencil in the other hand and sign their name. Most will groan or laugh as they proceed to scrawl their signatures.

Have everyone turn to a partner and answer:

● **How did you feel when I asked you to write your name with the other hand?** (Weird; challenged; embarrassed.)

● **How is that like dealing with change?** (It's awkward and uncomfortable at first; I did better than I thought.)

● What effect does working at adapting to change have on the outcome? (If you've ever broken your writing hand and had to relearn with the other, you find the more you do it, the more natural it becomes; you need to give things a chance because they may not turn out great the first few tries.)

Encourage partners to share discoveries with the whole group. Then have people turn to their partners again and name one change they feel their church needs to make when it comes to learning.

Appoint a scribe for the entire group who'll write the "change ideas" on newsprint for all to see. If some answers are the same, simply give them a checkmark each time they're mentioned.

Have people share their ideas for change. If there are lots of different ideas, divide into smaller groups to address each idea. Have groups discuss two things:

● What would be the awkward/uncomfortable/embarrassing aspects of this change?

● What are the benefits of "working at it" so change can come about and become the natural way of doing things?

Have groups report back and choose which two areas of change they'd like to begin working on.

QUICK-CHANGE ARTIST

For those who can't think of a thing to change about your church's education methods, try this.

Have partners introduce themselves and tell about a favorite class they've taken and why it was their favorite.

Have partners stand back to back and change one subtle thing about themselves. For example, take off a watch, remove an earring, or roll up a sleeve. Next tell them to turn around and guess what their partners changed.

Have them turn back to back, change two things, and repeat the process. Then have them turn back to back, change three things, and try to figure out their partners' changes.

Next have partners discuss:

● **How'd you feel as you were asked to change more and more things?** (Silly; stumped; challenged.)

● **How is that like looking for ways to change or improve what goes on in church education?** (It's hard to think of what to change because everything seems to be going okay; you may not realize there are that many possibilities for change; some change may be so subtle nobody would ever notice, while other changes could be quite dramatic.)

Invite pairs to share their discoveries. Together talk about change in the church. Refer to earlier sections of this chapter to spark discussion.

WHAT HAVE YOU GOT TO LOSE?

Tell a group: **I've got a valuable piece of advice, and I'll tell you that advice if someone's willing to pay me five dollars for it.**

The advice is worth it, you'll find out. And I'm not kidding. I will take your five dollars and won't give it back.

Listen for the group's response. Are they eager to hop up and pay? Do they hesitate? Do they grumble? Wait for one person to bring you five dollars.

Once a volunteer comes forward, thank that person for the five dollars. Hand that person a slip of paper with this advice written on it: "To master change, shift your paradigm from what you'll lose to what you'll gain." Ask if your volunteer would like to share the advice with the entire group. Then read it to the entire group.

Ask people to think about a change before them and what they could gain by making that change. Hand your volunteer a $10 bill and say: **Remember my advice: To master change, shift your paradigm from what you'll lose to what you'll gain.**

By this time the rest of the group will probably gasp or kick themselves for not coming forward. Use this as a fine teachable moment.

Find out why the one person came forward. Why did the others hold back? How is that like the way we look at change?

Write your advice in large letters for all to see. Create two columns on newsprint. Label one "What we'd lose" and the other "What we'd gain." Then say: **Think about our church's education—for children, youth, and adults; Sunday school; Bible classes; sermons. If we were to make revolutionary changes in these areas what are we afraid we'd lose?** Fill in all the responses in the loss column.

Next say: **Remember my advice? Let's look at what we'd gain.** Brainstorm and list the benefits of change.

Let this activity lead you into decisions and action for change.

TELL ABOUT A TIME

To get people comfortable talking about change, have partners each tell about a time they feared a change in their lives and what good came from that change.

Have group members analyze the similarities of the fears they had and the similarities of the good that came from the change.

Use this discussion as an entree into talking about needed change in the church. Talk about ways to help alleviate congregation members' fears and help them see the good that could come.

SMOOTH SAILING OR CRASHING AND BURNING

Hand out copies of the illustration on page 271. Explain the three stages of change that relate to the picture. Form groups no larger than four to discuss:

● **Where is our church in this picture? Why?**

● **Where should our church be in this picture? Why?**

● **What are specific instances when our church has chosen the "Path to Death"? the "Path to New Life"?**

● **What do we need to do to keep us moving toward life?**

OVERCOMING NAYSAYERS

Have fun with this role-play scenario on page 285. Form groups no larger than four. Give each person a slip of paper with one of the four roles on it. (If you have a group with fewer than four people just make sure "Role 1" gets assigned.)

Set up the scene. Say: **You're all on the church's education committee. The person assigned Role 1 will begin your discussion. After that you're on your own. You have about seven minutes.**

Let the role-play begin. Make sure you watch and listen for what goes on in the groups. (If you have enough people, you might want to appoint an observer for each group to jot down observations.)

After a few minutes, call the group back together. If people are unclear about what roles each person played, have everyone read their roles at this time. Debrief the experience. Ask:

● **If you had Role 1, how did you feel during that experience? Role 2? Role 3? Role 4?**

● **How is this experience like or unlike what happens in churches?**

● **What advice would you give someone in real life who's like Role 1? Role 2? Role 3? Role 4?**

● **How can we make our church a place where people learn to welcome change? What positive actions can we take to overcome "the naysayers"?**

Conclude with a group prayer. Join hands and have each person say a prayer for the people who really do feel like the people you role played.

Role 1: You're really excited about changing (choose only one of the following):

● your church's Sunday school curriculum.

● your church's approach to the sermon time; you'd like to see more creativity, energy, and involvement.

● your church's traditional adult Bible class that's been led by the same person for 10 years.

You want to get the others on your committee to buy into the revolutionary ideas for change you know will work. You have lots of sound reasons for advocating the change.

Role 2: You like things the way they are. Your motto is in cement: "We've always done it that way. And I like it that way!"

Role 3: You hate change, and you're downright pessimistic. You're sure anything new won't work. You're always vocal about the reasons it'll never work. You don't like to listen to what anyone else has to say.

Role 4: The real reason you don't like change is that you hate to rock the boat. You're more afraid of hurting someone's feelings than advocating anything that's not status quo. You're always worried about "What will so-and-so think?"

LOOK IN THE BOOK

Take time to explore Scripture. Use the Bible to learn about how God has worked through change in the past. Hold on to the promise that God never changes, but he sees us through anything. Remember the ultimate in change and a radical way of life: Jesus Christ!

Here's an assortment of verses to pique your interest. By no means are they exhaustive; they're just a beginning.

- Isaiah 43:1-19 (God has done great things for the people he made.)
- Malachi 3:6a (The Lord doesn't change.)
- Matthew 9:16-17 (Jesus talks about the danger of pouring new wine into old wineskins.)
- Romans 12:1-2 (Be changed within by a new way of thinking.)
- Hebrews 13:8 (Jesus is the same yesterday, today, and tomorrow.)
- Revelation 21:5 (God makes all things new.)

BUILD A SUPPORT NETWORK

Surround yourself with people who'll support and encourage you. Being a revolutionary isn't easy. You'll come up against a lot of obstacles. But like anyone who believes in a cause, you know it's worth it. So find people in your congregation, in your denomination, in your community. Have them join you in grappling with the dramatic changes that need to be made in overcoming why nobody learns much of anything at church. God be with you!

EPILOGUE

Education in the church is in trouble. But not by intentional design. We're in this mess because we've been programmed.

We are products of a failed educational system. We grew up with forgotten goals, r-bbits, trivial pursuits, and an overdose of passive learning. These approaches are so ingrained that we practice them without thinking. We're on autopilot.

But we cannot continue. We're losing too many souls. And we know better. We really do.

Stop and think about how you'd educate someone who'd come to work for you. Consider a newly hired secretary. You wouldn't attempt to train your new secretary with a pile of crosswords, fill-in-the-blanks, and hidden-word puzzles. You wouldn't scramble the word Macintosh to teach your secretary how to use the computer. You wouldn't insist your new secretary pore over the copy machine's users manual to find some worthless fact like the date it was invented. You wouldn't require your secretary to spend valuable time memorizing every church member's address and telephone number.

No, you know intuitively these silly methods will not help your secretary quickly and effectively learn the job. Common sense tells you there's a better way to educate your secretary.

It's time also to apply some common sense to all learning in the church. The remedies we've prescribed in this book are not eccentric, untested ideas. They're common sense approaches to learning that any church can utilize.

Now is the time for common sense, for courage, for change. We're faced with a world that desperately needs to learn—to learn about and become transformed by the saving grace of Jesus Christ.

ENDNOTES

INTRODUCTION

1. Barna, G. *What Americans Believe.* Ventura, CA: Regal Books, 1991, p. 280.

2. *Yearbook of American and Canadian Churches.* Nashville: Abingdon, 1994. The Statistical Abstract of the United States. Washington: U.S. Department of Commerce, 1992.

3. Chandler, R. *Racing Toward 2001.* Grand Rapids, MI: Zondervan, 1992, p. 112.

4. *Yearbook of American and Canadian Churches.* Nashville: Abingdon, 1990.

5. A Group Publishing poll of churchgoers, 1992.

6. Benson, P., and Eklin, C. *Effective Christian Education: A National Study of Protestant Congregations.* Summary Report. Minneapolis: Search Institute, 1990, p. 58.

7. Barna, G. *Ministry Currents,* October–December, 1991, p. 9.

8. Chandler, R. *Racing Toward 2001.* p. 112.

9. Author interview with a Sunday school student, 1992.

10. Benson, P., and Eklin C. *Effective Christian Education.* Summary Report. p. 2.

11. McNichol, T. *USA Weekend,* September 18, 1992, p. 5.

12. Carvajal, T. University of Northern Colorado, Greeley.

13. *The Wall Street Journal,* September 11, 1992, p. B1.

CHAPTER 1

1. Gardner, H. *The Unschooled Mind.* New York: Basic Books, 1991, p. 138.

2. Wood, G. *Schools That Work.* New York: Dutton, 1992, p. xx.

3. Ibid., p. xxi.

4. Gatto, J. *The Wall Street Journal,* July 25, 1991.

5. Quote from *The Brokaw Report,* NBC, August 29, 1992.

6. Wood, G. *Schools That Work.* p. 238.

7. *Effective Christian Education: A National Study of Protestant Congregations.* Minneapolis: Search Institute, 1990, p. 25.

8. Ibid., pp. 46-47.

9. Barna, G. *What Americans Believe.* Ventura, CA: Regal Books, 1991, p. 230.

CHAPTER 2

1. Healy, J. *Endangered Minds.* New York: Simon & Schuster, 1990, p. 20.

2. Ibid., pp. 20-21.

3. Stoddard, L. *Redesigning Education.* Tucson: Zephyr Press, 1992, p. 61.

4. Smith, F. *Insult to Intelligence.* Portsmouth, NH: Heinemann, 1988, p. 80.

5. Wood, G. *Schools That Work.* New York: Dutton, 1992, p. 128.

CHAPTER 3

1. Group Publishing national survey of 226 church-attending fifth- and sixth-graders, 1992.

2. Barna, G. *What Americans Believe*. Ventura, CA: Regal Books, 1991, p. 212.

3. *Effective Christian Education: A National Study of Protestant Congregations*. Minneapolis: Search Institute, 1990, pp. 26-27.

4. Ibid., p. 57.

5. Barna, G. *What Americans Believe*. p. 173.

6. Group Publishing national survey.

7. Wood, G. *Schools That Work*. New York: Dutton, 1992, p. 167.

8. Healy, J. *Endangered Minds*. New York: Simon & Schuster, 1990, p. 281.

9. Stevenson, H., and Stigler, J. *The Learning Gap*. New York: Summit Books, 1992, p. 195.

10. Wood, G. *Schools That Work*. p. 13.

11. Healy, J. *Endangered Minds*. p. 279.

CHAPTER 4

1. Healy, J. *Endangered Minds*. New York: Simon & Schuster, 1990, p. 27.

2. Stevenson, H., and Stigler, J. *The Learning Gap*. New York: Summit Books, 1992, p. 13.

3. Healy, J. *Endangered Minds*. p. 278.

4. Stoddard, L. *Redesigning Education*. Tucson: Zephyr Press, 1992, p. 55.

5. Stevenson, H., and Stigler, J. *The Learning Gap*. p. 213.

6. Smith, F. *Insult to Intelligence*. Portsmouth, NH: Heinemann, 1988, pp. 83, 261.

7. Perkins, D. *Smart Schools.* New York: The Free Press, 1992, p. 8.

CHAPTER 5

1. Stipp, D. *The Wall Street Journal,* September 11, 1992, p. B4.

2. Smith, F. *Insult to Intelligence.* Portsmouth, NH: Heinemann, 1988, p. 11.

3. *Effective Christian Education: A National Study of Protestant Congregations.* Minneapolis: Search Institute, 1990, p. 36.

4. Group Publishing national survey of 226 church-attending fifth- and sixth-graders, 1992.

5. Hendricks, H. *The 7 Laws of the Teacher.* Atlanta: Walk Thru the Bible Ministries, 1987, p. 66.

6. Healy, J. *Endangered Minds.* New York: Simon & Schuster, 1990, p. 96.

7. Perkins, D. *Smart Schools.* New York: The Free Press, 1992, p. 32.

8. Furnish, D. *Experiencing the Bible With Children.* Nashville: Abingdon, 1990, p. 124.

9. Udall, A., and Daniels, J. *Creating the Thoughtful Classroom.* Tucson: Zephyr Press, 1991, p. 73.

10. Ibid., p. 85.

11. *Effective Christian Education.* p. 36.

12. Healy, J. *Endangered Minds.* p. 295.

13. Ibid., adapted from pp. 295-296.

CHAPTER 6

1. Stoddard, L. *Redesigning Education.* Tucson: Zephyr Press, 1992, p. 14.

2. Manegold, C. *Newsweek,* December 2, 1991, p. 55.

3. Burns, J. *The Youth Builder.* Eugene, OR: Harvest House Publishers, 1988, p. 184.

4. Hendricks, H. *Teaching to Change Lives.* Portland, OR: Multnomah Press, 1987.

5. Naisbitt, J. *Trend Letter,* June 25, 1992, p. 3.

6. Atkins, A. *Child,* May, 1991, p. 102.

7. Quote from *20/20,* ABC, April 19, 1991.

8. Goleman, D., Kaufman, P., and Ray, M. *The Creative Spirit.* New York: Dutton, 1992, p. 43.

9. Woods, P. *What's a Christian?* Loveland, CO: Group Publishing, 1990, p. 1.

10. *Hands-On Bible Curriculum, 5th & 6th Grade,* Teachers Guide, Year B, Quarter 1, "Dealing With Disabilities/Airline Disaster Activity." Loveland, CO: Group Publishing, 1993.

11. Paulson, N. *Preschool Program: Loving God, Loving Others.* Loveland, CO: Group Publishing, 1992, pp. 122-124.

12. *Hands-On Bible Curriculum, 5th & 6th Grade,* Teachers Guide, Year B, Quarter 1, "This Little Light/Candle Gauntlet Activity." Loveland, CO: Group Publishing, 1993.

13. Chromey, R. *Turning Depression Upside Down.* Loveland, CO: Group Publishing, 1992, pp. 35-36.

14. Cassidy, D. *Faith for Tough Times.* Loveland, CO: Group Publishing, 1991, pp. 26-27.

15. Kelly, P. *Forgiveness.* Loveland, CO: Group Publishing, 1992, pp. 40-41.

CHAPTER 7

1. Stevenson, H., and Stigler, J. *The Learning Gap.* New York: Summit Books, 1992, p. 70.

2. McCabe, M., and Rhoades, J. "Developing Higher-Level Thinking Skills Through Cooperative Learning Strategies," ASCD Annual Conference, San Francisco, CA, March 17, 1991.

3. Goodlad, J. *A Place Called School.* New York: McGraw-Hill, 1984.

4. Healy, J. *Endangered Minds.* New York: Simon & Schuster, 1990, p. 96.

5. Steinberg, A. *Education Letter,* Harvard University Press, November/December, 1989, p. 1.

6. Hardel, D. *Who Is Jesus?* Loveland, CO: Group Publishing, 1991, pp. 15-16.

7. *Hands-On Bible Curriculum, 5th & 6th Grade,* Teachers Guide, Year A, Quarter 4, "Hidden Messages Activity." Loveland, CO: Group Publishing, 1993.

8. *Quick Devotions for Children's Ministry.* Loveland, CO: Group Publishing, 1990, p. 71.

9. *Hands-On Bible Curriculum, 5th & 6th Grade,* Teachers Guide, Year A, Quarter 3. Loveland, CO: Group Publishing, 1992.

10. Ibid., p. 108.

CHAPTER 8

1. Hendricks, H. *The 7 Laws of the Teacher.* Atlanta: Walk Thru the Bible Ministries, 1987, p. 88.

2. Wood, G. *Schools That Work.* New York: Dutton, 1992, p. 153.

3. Conlin, E. *INC.,* July, 1991, p. 65.

4. Goleman, D., Kaufman, P., and Ray, M. *The*

Creative Spirit. New York: Dutton, 1992, p. 90.

5. Wood, G. *Schools That Work.* p. 168.

6. Sizer, T. *Horace's School.* New York: Houghton Mifflin, 1992, p. 99.

7. Keffer, L. *Sunday School Specials.* Loveland, CO: Group Publishing, 1992, pp. 30-33.

CHAPTER 9

1. Roehlkepartain, J. *Youth Ministry: Its Impact on Church Growth.* Loveland, CO: Group Publishing, 1989, p. 7.

2. Hull, J. *What Prevents Christian Adults From Learning?* Philadelphia: Trinity Press International, 1991, p. 65.

3. Boylan, B. *What's Your Point?* New York: Warner Books, 1988, p. 80.

4. Wilkinson, B. *The 7 Laws of the Learner.* Sisters, OR: Multnomah Press, 1992, p. 32.

5. Udall, A., and Daniels, J. *Creating the Thoughtful Classroom.* Tucson: Zephyr Press, 1991, p. 66.

6. Hinchey, D. *5-Minute Messages for Children.* Loveland, CO: Group Publishing, 1992, p. 13.

7. Ibid., pp. 22-23.

CHAPTER 10

1. Barna, G. *The Frog in the Kettle.* Ventura, CA: Regal Books, 1990, pp. 21-22.

2. Wood, G. *Schools That Work.* New York: Dutton, 1992, p. 10.

3. Barna, G. *User Friendly Churches.* Ventura, CA: Regal Books, 1991, p. 176.

4. *USA Today,* November 24, 1992.

5. Benson, P., and Eklin, C. *Effective Christian Education: A National Study of Protestant Congregations.* Summary Report. Minneapolis: Search Institute, 1990, p. 67.

RECOMMENDED RESOURCES

Active Bible Curriculum. Loveland, CO: Group Publishing, 1990-1994. A series of four-week courses, each on a different topic, for junior high and senior high students. Reproducible handouts.

Apply-It-To-Life Bible Curriculum. Loveland, CO: Group Publishing, 1995, 1996. Four-week courses for adults, using age-appropriate active and interactive learning techniques.

Baker, Brant. *Let the Children Come.* Minneapolis: Augsburg, 1991. Creative, active children's sermons.

Barna, George. *The Frog in the Kettle.* Ventura, CA: Regal Books, 1990. Research and interpretation for local churches.

Barna, George. *What Americans Believe.* Ventura, CA: Regal Books, 1991. Research and insights on religious beliefs and values.

Bauer, Karen, and Drew, Rosa. *Alternatives to Worksheets.* Cypress, CA: Creative Teaching Press, 1992. Creative methods to illustrate themes and concepts.

Beating Boredom With Active Learning. Loveland, CO: Group Publishing, 1990. A 30-minute teacher-training video showing an actual high school Bible class using active learning.

Belasco, James. *Teaching the Elephant to Dance.* New York: Penguin Books. A guide for empowering change in organizations.

Benson, Peter, and Eklin, Carolyn. *Effective Christian Education: A National Study of Protestant Congregations.* Minneapolis: Search Institute, 1990. A summary of the landmark study of Christian education in six denominations.

Children's Ministry That Works. Loveland, CO: Group Publishing, 1991. Practical tips for starting or revitalizing a children's ministry.

Dodd, Anne Wescott. *A Parent's Guide to Innovative Education.* Chicago: The Noble Press, 1992. An explanation of needed reforms in the schools.

Flinn, Lisa, and Younger, Barbara. *Making Scripture Stick.* Loveland, CO: Group Publishing, 1992. Active experiences to help children understand various Scriptures.

Fun Group-Involving Skits. Loveland, CO: Group Publishing, 1993. A collection of meaningful scripts that involve entire groups in the action.

Fun-to-Learn Bible Lessons. Loveland, CO: Group Publishing, 1993-1995. A series of age-level books with active lessons for preschoolers through upper-elementary.

Furnish, Dorothy Jean. *Experiencing the Bible With Children.* Nashville: Abingdon, 1990. Multi-sensory teaching ideas.

Hands-On Bible Curriculum. Loveland, CO: Group Publishing. Quarterly Sunday school curriculum utilizing active and interactive learning. Consists of a teachers guide and a Learning Lab box filled with creative classroom learning gizmos.

Healy, Jane. *Endangered Minds.* New York: Simon & Schuster, 1990. A scholarly approach to problems and solutions in contemporary education.

Helping Children Know God. Loveland, CO: Group Publishing, 1995. Five-senses learning to build kids' faith.

Hinchey, Donald. *5-Minute Messages for Children.* Loveland, CO: Group Publishing, 1992. Creative children's sermons.

Hinchey, Donald. *5-Minute Messages for Children's Special Days.* Loveland, CO: Group Publishing, 1994. Active messages for holidays, birthdays, and anniversaries.

Hinchey, Donald. *6-Minute Messages for Children.* Loveland, CO: Group Publishing, 1993. More creative, active children's sermons.

Keffer, Lois. *Sunday School Specials, Volumes 1, 2, and 3.* Loveland, CO: Group Publishing, 1992-1995. Active lessons for combined-age groups.

Lively Bible Lessons. Loveland, CO: Group Publishing, 1991, 1992. A series of books with active lessons for preschoolers and elementary-age children.

Nappa, Mike and Amy. *Bore No More.* Loveland, CO: Group Publishing, 1995. Creative ideas to make sermons active, interactive, and effective.

Parolini, Stephen and Lauffer, Lisa Baba. *Fun Bible-Learning Projects for Young Teenagers.* Loveland, CO: Group Publishing, 1995. Over 100 hands-on activities.

Projects With a Purpose. Loveland, CO: Group Publishing, 1993-1994. Four-week courses that engage young people in meaningful projects such as research, video production, and a prayer concert.

Real Life Bible Curriculum. Loveland, CO: Group Publishing, 1995, 1996. Active and interactive sessions for teenagers, based on 24 core Christian beliefs.

Schultz, Thom and Joani. *Do It! Active Learning in Youth Ministry.* Loveland, CO: Group Publishing, 1989. A thorough explanation of active learning plus a collection of active-learning experiences.

Smith, Cindy. *Amazing Stories From Genesis.* Loveland, CO: Group Publishing, 1992. Active-learning lessons for grades three and four.

Smith, Frank. *Insult to Intelligence.* Portsmouth, NH: Heinemann Educational Books, 1988. A condemnation of the "drill and kill" approach to education.